WARRIOR • 158

# PIRATE:
# THE GOLDEN AGE

**A KONSTAM & D RICKMAN**

**ILLUSTRATED BY G RAVA**

*Series editor* Marcus Cowper

First published in Great Britain in 2011 by Osprey Publishing
Midland House, West Way, Botley, Oxford OX2 0PH, UK
44-02 23rd St, Suite 219, Long Island City, NY 11101, USA
E-mail: info@ospreypublishing.com

OSPREY PUBLISHING IS PART OF THE OSPREY GROUP

A CIP catalog record for this book is available from the British Library

Print ISBN: 978 1 84908 497 0

PDF e-book ISBN: 978 1 84908 498 7

EPUB e-book ISBN: 978 1 84908 941 8

Editorial by Ilios Publishing Ltd, Oxford, UK (www.iliospublishing.com)
Page layout by: Mark Holt
Index by Marie-Pierre Evans
Typeset in Sabon and Myriad Pro
Originated by Blenheim Colour, UK
Printed in China through Worldprint Ltd

11  12  13  14  15    10 9 8 7 6 5 4 3 2 1

www.ospreypublishing.com

## AUTHORS' NOTE

The book is a collaborative venture, the first between us since we wrote
and illustrated our first Osprey book some 18 years ago. Since then I
(Angus) have specialised in the history of piracy, and have written several
books on the subject, including *Piracy: The Complete History* for Osprey
Publishing. The biggest problem was trying to unravel the myth from the
reality, scraping away the layers of later interpretation to reveal the real
pirates who terrorised the waters of the Caribbean and the Americas almost
exactly three centuries ago. The trouble was that our enduring image of
pirates of this time is coloured by the works of Robert Louis Stevenson,
J. M. Barrie and Raphael Sabatini. They created the pirate myths of walking
the plank, burying treasure and maps where 'X' marks the spot.

A new layer of pirate mythology was provided by Hollywood, where the
portrayal of pirates by actors from Errol Flynn to Johnny Depp drew on the
rakish illustrations of pirates produced by late 19th- and early 20th-century
artists like Howard Pyle. The few illustrations available showing the real
pirates and sailors of the Golden Age of Piracy were largely ignored. Since
our first collaboration, David Rickman has become a leading military
illustrator and an expert on historical clothing. However, as a resident of
Pyle's home town of Wilmington, Delaware, he found himself intrigued by
Pyle's portrayal of pirates, and how they altered our perception of pirate
appearance. Pyle created a 'pirate look' that bore little resemblance to the
real thing. We had both been trying the same thing from two different
directions – one trying to separate pirate fact from fiction using historical
sources, and the other through a scholarly study of pirate clothing. It was a
collaboration that was meant to be, and this book is the result.

## ARTIST'S NOTE

## EDITOR'S NOTE

All images in this book are from the authors' own collections.

## THE WOODLAND TRUST

Osprey Publishing are supporting the Woodland Trust, the UK's leading
woodland conservation charity, by funding the dedication of trees.

# CONTENTS

# PIRATE
# THE GOLDEN AGE

## INTRODUCTION

The term 'The Golden Age of Piracy' is accepted by most pirate historians as a historical shorthand, although its chronological definition is loosely defined. The term itself was never used until the 1920s, when Rafael Sabatini penned the pirate novels *Captain Blood* and *The Black Swan*, which would later be adapted into swashbuckling films. The term was used with a sense of irony, as even Sabatini would admit that there was nothing romantic about piracy. It was, after all, merely a form of violent crime committed on the high seas. However, as a historical term, it serves the useful purpose of encompassing the great upsurge of piratical activity that took place during the first decades of the 18th century.

Some historians place it between the 1690s and the 1730s, but I favour a tighter historical span, a mere decade, from 1714 until 1724. Its end is marked by the publication of the mysterious Captain Charles Johnson's A *General History of the Robberies and Murders of the Most Notorious Pyrates* (referred to hereafter as *A General History*), which provided readers with a sensational account of the lives of some of the most notorious pirates of the previous decade, including Blackbeard, Bartholomew Roberts, and the female pirates Anne Bonny and Mary Read. This was the era when the most famous pirates in history made their mark, and where, from Johnson on, fiction began to draw away from fact. The aim of this book is to reveal as best we can the reality of pirate life and their appearance during this turbulent decade.

## CHRONOLOGY

### 1713
| | |
|---|---|
| April | The Treaty of Utrecht ends Britain's involvement in the War of the Spanish Succession (1701–14). |
| November | Benjamin Hornigold establishes a pirate base on New Providence in the Bahamas. |

### 1715
| | |
|---|---|
| June | Spanish treasure fleet wrecked off eastern coast of Florida. |

## 1716

**January**        Henry Jennings launches raid on Spanish salvage camp.

**September**      Sam Bellamy leaves Hornigold and begins own cruise.

## 1717

**February**       Bellamy captures the *Whydah*.

**April**          Stede Bonnet begins his cruise. The *Whydah* is wrecked off Cape Cod, and Bellamy is lost at sea.

**June**           Blackbeard leaves Hornigold and begins own cruise.

**July**           New Providence is now a major pirate base.

**September**      British government offers a pardon to pirates.

**November**       Blackbeard captures *La Concorde*, renaming it as *Queen Anne's Revenge*.

## 1718

**May**            Blackbeard blockades Charles Town (Charleston), South Carolina.

**July**           Governor Woodes Rogers establishes British rule in the Bahamas.

| | |
|---|---|
| September | Blackbeard uses Ocracoke Island, North Carolina, as a base. |
| | Stede Bonnet captured in Cape Fear River. |
| | Howell Davis mutinies and turns pirate. |
| November | Blackbeard attacked and killed in battle off Ocracoke. |

## 1719

| | |
|---|---|
| February | Richard Worley hanged in Williamsburg, Virginia. |
| March | Blackbeard's crew hanged at Williamsburg. |
| April | Christopher Condent establishes a pirate base on St Mary's Island, Madagascar. |
| May | Bartholomew Roberts joins Davis' crew. |
| June | Davis killed on Principe, off West Africa. Roberts assumes command. |
| October | Roberts captures Portuguese treasure galleon off Bahia, Brazil. |
| November | Bonnet and his crew are hanged in Charles Town, South Carolina. |
| | Walter Kennedy defects from Roberts' crew and begins his own cruise. |

## 1720

| | |
|---|---|
| March | Charles Vane hanged in Jamaica. |
| August | Jack Rackam, Anne Bonny and Mary Read begin their cruise. |
| | Edward England captures East Indiaman in Indian Ocean. |
| October | Condent captures East Indiaman in Indian Ocean. |
| November | Rackam caught and hanged in Jamaica. His two female accomplices are spared execution. |
| | Kennedy shipwrecked on western coast of Scotland. |

## 1721

| | |
|---|---|
| January | Many of Kennedy's crew are hanged in Leith, outside Edinburgh. |
| April | Thomas Anstis defects from Roberts and begins his own cruise. |
| | England deposed and replaced by John Taylor. |

| | |
|---|---|
| May | George Lowther mutinies and begins his cruise. |
| July | Kennedy and his remaining crew are hanged in London. |
| November | Edward Low mutinies and begins his cruise. |
| **1722**<br>February | Roberts is killed in battle with a Royal Navy warship, and his ships are captured. |
| March | Lowther disappears from the record; it is possible that he committed suicide. |
| April | Roberts' crew are hanged at Cape Coast Castle, West Africa. |
| **1723**<br>May | Taylor surrenders in Panama, and walks free. |
| | Charles Harris and his crew are hanged in Newport, Rhode Island. |
| **1724**<br>January | Low disappears from the record; it is possible that he was marooned by his crew. |
| May | Captain Charles Johnson publishes *A General History*. |
| November | John Gow mutinies and begins his cruise. |
| **1725**<br>February | Gow is captured in Orkney. |
| June | Gow and his crew are hanged in London. His exploits are included in new edition of Johnson's *A General History*. |

# RECRUITMENT

Becoming a pirate was not a straightforward business – very few seamen of the early 18th century actually set out to be pirates. The usual way it happened was that seamen mutinied against their captain, were captured by pirates and elected to join them, or else found their way to a pirate haven and joined a crew. Probably the only exception was Stede Bonnet, the gentleman plantation owner from Barbados, who, suffering a mid-life crisis, bought his own sloop, hired a questionable crew, and so established himself as a pirate captain. For Bonnet, the allure was a romantic vision of piracy and an escape from the monotony of colonial life. He had the money, if not the skill, to indulge in his piratical fantasy, and ultimately he paid for his decision with his life.

Many of the pirates who began their careers in New Providence in the Bahamas were former privateers. When the Treaty of Utrecht brought an end to British involvement in the War of the Spanish Succession (1701–14) in the

One of the most common grievances of merchant seamen during the early 18th century was a lack of provisions. Therefore the lifestyle of a pirate crew, able to forage where they will, and steal food from victims, had a significant appeal. This seaman of the period is catching a turtle, a useful source of food in Caribbean waters.

spring of 1713, hundreds of former privateersmen found themselves out of work. While a few operated from British-owned ports in North America or the West Indies, a large minority were based in Port Royal, Jamaica. While many of these seamen turned to poorly paid legitimate work, others cast around for something more lucrative.

Their opportunity came in late June 1715, when a Spanish treasure fleet was caught by a hurricane and wrecked off the coast of Florida. The Spanish sent a salvage team from Havana to rescue what treasure they could, but others had the same idea. Led by a privateer, Captain Henry Jennings, a group of around 300 British former privateersmen raided the salvage camp and made off with a fortune in silver coins. As Britain and Spain were at peace with each other this could be construed as a hostile act, so the Governor of Jamaica distanced himself from the raid. Jennings and his men simply moved to New Providence and established a base there that was closer to the wreck sites and beyond the reach of the British authorities. Jennings repeated the raid a few months later, and captured even more plunder from the Spanish.

This meant that by the spring of 1716 the island of New Providence had become a makeshift haven for those operating outside the law. Many of these former privateers turned to piracy, although many still refused to attack British ships, concentrating their acts on their 'natural enemies' the French and the Spanish. Inevitably, this pirate haven attracted other criminals, as well as unscrupulous merchants, tavern keepers, prostitutes and so on – everything a pirate shanty town needed to thrive. The biggest upsurge in pirate numbers in a century had come about through a combination of unemployment and opportunity.

This was an exceptional chain of events. After 1715, for a decade, the only similar haven to New Providence was St Mary's Isle (now Isle St Marie), off the north-eastern coast of Madagascar. Even then this pirate base was far from the busy shipping lanes, save for those used by well-armed East Indiamen, whose crews were highly unlikely to join the pirates. Still, merchant ships arrived at the island to trade with the pirates there, and there was always the possibility that some of these trading ships would provide fresh recruits. The biggest influx of new blood probably came in April 1698, when the pirate hunter William Kidd arrived off the island in the *Adventure Galley*. Despite the claims of the East India Company, Kidd was no pirate, but he knew that the trading company viewed him as such. In order to clear his name he planned to attack the pirate haven, but instead his men mutinied and elected to join the pirates. By the 1720s St Mary's Isle was a dilapidated shell of a settlement, as most of its piratical population had either moved away or been captured.

The end of New Providence as a pirate haven was even more spectacular. In August 1718 Governor Woodes Rogers arrived there in order to establish British authority over the Bahamas, backed by the guns of Royal Naval warships. While Charles Vane and a few other die-hard pirates fled to continue their depredations, the rest acquiesced and accepted a pardon. This pardon was part of a new 'carrot-and-stick' policy. It helped rid the seas of many of the less virulent pirates, and allowed the Royal Navy to concentrate its efforts against the few who remained at large. By the late summer of 1718 probably less than a dozen pirate ships and crews remained at large in the waters of the Americas.

Of course, several of the pirates who accepted a pardon eventually resumed their piratical activities, either by recruiting like-minded seamen in New Providence or other ports, or through mutiny. Those who chose the first option – men like 'Calico Jack' Rackam – were essentially opportunistic, small-time pirates, who tended to be caught before they could cause much damage. Rackam would hardly be remembered at all were it not for the two women who served aboard his ship – Anne Bonny and Mary Read. Like the rest of their shipmates they were recruited in the taverns of New Providence. Despite the establishment of British rule, few places in the world could boast a higher percentage of former pirates amongst their population, and inevitably some of these men – and women – were simply waiting for an opportunity to become pirates again.

Throughout the so-called Golden Age of Piracy the majority of pirates were recruited through mutiny or capture. The result was a thread of crime, where a crew would mutiny, and then capture other ships and recruit more men. While some pirate crews might split into factions, they all tended to repeat this process. Therefore, for each mutiny during this period, the chances were

Most pirates started out following more mundane occupations related to the sea. Shown here is the Newfoundland fishery in the late 17th century, a rich hunting ground for the pirate Bartholomew Roberts.

that a pirate crew would be created, then continue to grow, divide and grow again until all the various splinter groups could be tracked down and captured.

A prime example is provided by Howell Davis, who led a mutiny on board two Bahamian sloops in September 1718. Most of his shipmates were ex-pirates, and these men began a long-running thread of piratical activity. Whenever he captured ships he tried to recruit some of the crew. In May 1719 the pirates took the *Princess* of London, and once again he recruited more men. One of these was Bartholomew Roberts (or 'Black Bart'), who assumed the captaincy after Davis' death a few months later.

Roberts then repeated the process in the Caribbean, despite the division of his crew when a rival – Walter Kennedy – made off with his flagship. Roberts' piratical reign of terror continued until January 1722, when his ship was outfought and captured by HMS *Swallow* off the West African coast. During these intervening years he continued to recruit more men, while the splinter group formed by Kennedy did the same, until his shipwreck and capture in Scotland in late 1720.

By then other splinter groups had broken away from Roberts' crew, and the same pattern repeated itself. Thomas Anstis, one of the original mutineers, parted company from Roberts in April 1721, while commanding a small sloop. That year he captured several ships in the Caribbean, recruiting more crew as he did so, but in August 1722 most of his men were captured in the Cayman Islands. Anstis escaped in a sloop, and continued cruising until he was shot by his own men, who then turned themselves over to the Dutch authorities on Curaçao in June 1723. Thus a trail of mutiny, recruitment and fragmentation that had lasted for almost five years finally came to an end. During this time the original group of 60 mutineers had widened their piratical circle to embrace as many as 300 others.

Of course, not all mutineers or pirate recruits were necessarily volunteers. According to Captain Johnson (1726), the Orcadian pirate John Gow began his career by leading a mutiny against an overbearing captain. According to Daniel Defoe (1725) there were seven mutineers on board, and on the evening of 3 November 1724 they held the watch on deck at gunpoint while they murdered the Captain and three of his officers, before throwing the bodies over the side. Then they 'threatened the rest with death if they stirred from their hammocks, so that there was not the least opposition offered. When all was over, all hands were called upon deck, and Gow declared himself Captain, and said to them, "If hereafter I see any of you whispering together you shall be served in the same manner, as those that are gone before". They then set about their piratical ventures.'

These men were therefore coerced into piracy, as no doubt were many members of mutinous crews. In May 1721, when the crew of the slave ship *Gambia Castle* mutinied and stole their ship at anchor in the river Gambia, their ringleader George Lowther addressed the crew and told them that what they had done was a capital crime, so any thoughts of returning home were pure folly. Like it or not, the mutineers were forced to turn to piracy. That same year a row broke out between a captain and the crew of a longboat while loading a cargo of logwood in the Bay of Honduras. One of them, Ned Low, picked up a musket and fired at the captain, but missed him and hit a man standing next to him. Officially, the entire 13-man crew of the longboat were branded as mutineers, and had no choice but to flee the scene. As Johnson put it: 'The next day they took a small vessel, and go in her, make a black flag, and declare war against all the world.'

The same coercion was less apparent amongst the crew of a ship captured by pirates. The pirates effectively offered them the choice to join them, but many seamen preferred to remain on the right side of the law. After all, once branded a pirate they would almost certainly never have a chance to see their homes and families again. When Bartholomew Roberts was given this choice

Piracy, by its very nature, favoured recruits who were skilled seamen. Most though were considerably younger than the fictitious pirate portrayed here by Howard Pyle.

in May 1719 he joined Howell Davis' crew, but, according to Johnson, 'In the beginning he was averse to this sort of life, and would certainly have escaped from them, had a fair opportunity presented itself.'

This suggests coercion, and certainly in most pirate trials the most common defence by pirate crewmen was that they had been forced to join the pirate band and had subsequently never had an opportunity to escape. This defence tended to work only for the very young, or those captured by the authorities before they had had a chance to commit any crime. We will look at the psychology of piracy later – here we need merely to note that some pirates were clearly more committed than others, and that not all recruits joined the pirates willingly. Others though embraced the opportunity to cut their ties with authority, and eagerly threw in their lot with their captors.

## SKILLS

It can almost be taken for granted that all pirates were skilled and fully trained seamen. According to research carried out into the lives of European sailors of the early 18th century (Earle, 1998), the vast majority of sailors in merchant naval service were trained seamen – only the Royal Navy relied upon a quota of untrained 'landsmen' on board their warships to make up numbers. The theory behind this was that even the rawest of landlubbers could be trained sufficiently to form part of a gun crew, or to pull on a rope when ordered. The captains of merchant ships could be choosier about who they hired, and consequently all but the youngest ship's boys could usually 'hand, reef and steer'.

According to William Falconer's *Universal Dictionary of the Marine*, of 1769: 'The principal articles required in a common sailor to entitle him to full wages are that he can steer, sound, and manage the sails, by extending, reefing and furling them as occasion requires. When expert at these exercises, his skill in all other matters is taken for granted.' In other words, almost all sailors with a reasonable degree of experience behind them had the skills needed to help sail a ship, whether it be a merchant vessel or a pirate ship.

**A**

### RECRUITMENT

Pirate crews needed frequent replenishing. Most pirates were volunteers, but casualties from combat, disease, accidents and occasional desertions took their toll. So pirates took every opportunity they could to acquire new men. Since able seamen, maritime carpenters, coopers and navigators were preferred, it was sensible for pirates to seek recruits from among the crews of the ships they took as prizes. Here a pirate crew boards a merchant vessel that has surrendered after some resistance. Pirates did not like risking injuries to themselves or their prizes, so the captains or owners of ships that ran or fought were frequently punished. For the rest of the men, pirates tried persuasion first. The pirate quartermaster or captain might offer them arguments much along the lines of Bartholomew Roberts' well-known statement that 'In an honest service there is thin commons, low wages, and hard labour. In this [piracy], plenty and satiety.' And in truth, merchant crews were often overworked, underpaid and unhappy. Other arguments might include praise for the democratic life of piracy, the promise of better food, clothing and accommodation, liquor and, of course, wealth. For the potential recruits to accept these reasons, the pirates themselves would need to be better dressed and nourished than them, which argues against the popular image of pirates as gaunt and ragged vagabonds. Of course, if time was short or their arguments unconvincing, the pirates would then resort to force in order to fill out their crews.

These were the men who formed the crews of ships captured by pirates, or formed the backbone of mutinous crews. If they lacked the basics of seamanship, then they were less likely to be accepted by their fellow sailors, either as mutineers or as pirate recruits. Then again, a small proportion of merchant and pirate crews were made up of boys, most in their early teens, but with some as young as seven or eight. These children were divided into two groups: servants, who cleaned the cabins, washed dishes and served meals to the ship's officers and senior non-commissioned men, and ship's boys, who were effectively apprentices, training to become fully fledged seamen. Inevitably, a number of these inexperienced youngsters joined the ranks of pirate crews, and effectively they continued to serve their apprenticeship, albeit in a less structured environment.

In the merchant fleet of the period there was a distinct hierarchy of seamen, based upon experience and position. We have already mentioned the landsmen and boys at the bottom rung of the ladder. The bulk of a crew were experienced 'ordinary seamen', but the best of them aspired to becoming foremast men, who effectively acted as team leaders, supervising the day-to-day tasks of seamanship that were part of the everyday routine of a ship. On board the larger ocean-going merchant ships there was usually about one foremast man to every five or six ordinary seamen. On smaller vessels the hierarchy was less defined, with experienced men rated ordinary and other foretop men serving as the equivalent of warrant officers. On most ocean-going vessels with a crew of ten or more a boatswain served as a foreman for the seamen on board, and supervised all tasks requiring knowledge of seamanship. Effectively, he represented the next rung of the ladder.

On large ships – those with a crew of two dozen or so – the boatswain was usually assisted by foremast men rated as boatswain's mates. These were the cream of the crop – the most experienced foremast men in the ship. One of these might be rated as coxwain, in charge of the ship's boats. Another non-commissioned rank on board that was the equivalent of a boatswain was the gunner, responsible for maintaining the ship's armament and training the crew in their use. In most merchant ships this wasn't a full-time job, so often the gunner doubled as the boatswain, or as one of his mates. On larger ships, and especially on privateers, the gunner would have gunner's mates to assist him. Then there was the quartermaster. On a merchant ship he supervised the helmsman and was in charge of recording the vessel's course and speed. In pirate crews the quartermaster was something different – the equivalent of a second-in-command to the captain.

There were other specialized jobs on board a typical merchant ship, such as carpenter, sailmaker, ship's cook, captain's clerk, purser and sometimes surgeon, although the latter was more often merely someone with the 18th-century equivalent of a first-aid course and a medical chest. On larger ships these specialists had mates, or assistants, or more accurately apprentices. The largest vessels might also carry a cooper, and a steward or two to serve the captain and his officers. Apart from the carpenter, all of these jobs were held by men who were artisans in their own right, and therefore they might not necessarily be trained seamen. A young seaman might work his way up the hierarchy

A detail from the contemporary support and cartouche to the arms of Lord Aylmer, showing a sailor of the early 18th century carrying a navigational quadrant, which marks him as a seaman of some learning. His appearance is typical of seamen of the Golden Age of Piracy.

In the background of this imagined portrait of Captain George Lowther his men careen their ship on an isolated shore to clean and repair the hull. Pirate crews needed skilled boatswains and carpenters to carry out such tasks. The artist imagined that pirate captains dressed as gentlemen. The pirates next to him are dressed as common seamen, wearing a tricorne hat, a fur cap and a small, round hat. Notice also the entire absence of headscarves and earrings.

to become a boatswain, but he was unlikely to become a carpenter, sailmaker or suchlike unless he was chosen as an assistant to one on board. Obviously, these specialists were better paid than ordinary seamen, and their mates were ranked as the equivalent of foremast men.

In many cases these people were less willing than ordinary seamen to join a pirate gang if they were given the opportunity. They had moved up the hierarchical ladder, and many had dependants waiting for them back home. However, these specialists were exactly the kind of recruits most pirate crews needed, and so there are numerous cases of specialists such as carpenters, sailmakers or ship's surgeons being forced to join a pirate crew. It was also a matter of age. While most seamen were in their teens or twenties, those who held posts on board tended to be slightly older, usually in their late twenties or early thirties. Few mariners of the period were older than 40, although there were exceptions. Piracy appealed more to the younger crewmen, and to those lower down the hierarchical ladder.

On board a pirate ship the evidence suggests that this hierarchy was maintained, at least to some extent, and so a foremast man who joined a pirate crew would retain his rating. Also, while all crewmen were considered equal, some were more equal than others. This was particularly true when it came to those who held more responsible ranks, or who were specialists in their field. This is reflected in Bartholomew Roberts' articles (the rules by which pirates governed themselves), which directly mention the structure on board when speaking about the division of plunder: 'The Captain and Quartermaster to receive two shares of a prize; the Master, Boatswain and Gunner one share and a half, and other officers one and a quarter.'

Above these specialists were the ship's officers. On most merchantmen these were the captain himself and the mate. On larger ships there might be two or more mates, although usually only the first and second mate were considered to be officers. This hierarchy was different in the Royal Navy and the East India Company, but few pirates were directly recruited from these organisations, so for clarity we should remain with the system used by the majority of British and indeed other European seafarers, and by the crews of most colonial merchant vessels. In large ships, a master, in charge of navigation and seamanship, might act as a second-in-command, above the first mate. An ambitious and enterprising sailor could work his way up through the hierarchy, to become a boatswain, a gunner or even a second mate. But beyond that he would need a degree of education that was not usually available to most seamen of the period.

To be a captain, a master or a first mate, a seaman needed to be educated enough to navigate, deal with ship's paperwork and in many cases be numerate enough to hold his own in business transactions. A first mate was effectively an understudy to the captain, able to take over the job if his superior died or became incapacitated through injury or illness. Surprisingly, the majority of sailors had some schooling, and many knew the basics of writing and possibly had some arithmetic. Most of those who held an office on board – the boatswain, carpenter, mate, etc. – were literate enough to sign their own names, and sailors in general were more literate as a group than the average population on land. However, it took more than a basic knowledge of numeracy and literacy to navigate a ship.

Much has been made of the egalitarian nature of pirate crews, with the captain and the quartermaster elected by the crew. As in a merchant ship, a pirate captain had to navigate the vessel, maintain order amongst his crew, and make decisions about where the ship would go and what it would do. The quartermaster was his deputy, but he had a direct responsibility to supervise the division of plunder and to maintain discipline on board. Both of these men had to be able to navigate, which at the very least meant being able to determine latitude and longitude. The first was determined by taking a noon observation, and the second by estimating course and speed based on the three key tools of navigation – the compass, the traverse board (where time and course were recorded) and the log (to record speed through the water). The calculation of all this involved a degree of numeracy that was rare amongst seamen of the period.

This meant that while a pirate crew might be egalitarian, a captain could only really be chosen from a small pool of men – those who were literate and knew how to navigate. Obviously, standards varied, and in many cases the pool of potential seamen was so small as to make the choice of captain and quartermaster a simple one; anyone on board who could understand the basics of navigation was considered suitable material for command, as long as he had the charisma needed to retain his position. Some, like Charles Vane, didn't have what was needed, and were deposed. Others, like Blackbeard, held their command through a combination of intelligence, intimidation and cunning, and went on to be some of the most successful pirates in history.

# APPEARANCE

The popular image of pirates today – headscarves, earrings and flowing sashes included – is recognized and loved around the world. For many this 'pirate look' is the epitome of outlaw cool, and its influence is seen everywhere. However, the truth is that it never existed in history.

We must start by understanding that no eyewitness images of pirates and precious few first-hand descriptions survive from this period. Even those familiar 'portraits' of famous captains from *A General History* were by illustrators who never saw their subjects and whose job was to create exciting pictures, not authentic ones. In fact, these portraits evolved through various editions as the printing plates were repaired, recopied or replaced: Blackbeard changes hats, bandoliers, poses and costumes, while the differences between the English version of Mary Read and Ann Bonny and the Dutch version – from dowdy matrons in pantaloons to vixens in open shirts – is in more than one way revealing.

Our most familiar descriptions of pirates are also found in A *General History* and, like the illustrations, they mostly concern the battle dress of notably flamboyant captains:

> [Bartholomew] Roberts himself made a gallant figure, at the time of the engagement, being dressed in a rich crimson waistcoat and breeches, a red feather in his hat, a gold chain round his neck, with a diamond cross hanging to it, a sword in his hand, and two pairs of pistols hanging at the end of a silk sling flung over his shoulders, according to the custom of the pirates.

For all we know, descriptions such as this could be complete inventions, since they are not confirmed by any other sources. At the very best, they are second-hand accounts that probably tell us little about the clothing and arms of most pirate officers and their crews.

Because we have so little direct and reliable evidence, we must approach the question of how pirates dressed not only through research but also reason. We know that pirates were generally experienced seamen, and that most of their time was spent not in fighting or even swaggering but in performing the shipboard duties common to other sailors. Reason tells us then that, since there is no evidence to the contrary, pirates must have dressed in the same kinds of practical clothing as other seamen of their time. This idea is supported by eyewitness testimony from the 1720 trial of Read and Bonny. Describing their attack on her fishing boat, the owner recalled that the two women pirates 'were then on board the said sloop, and wore men's jackets and long trousers, and handkerchiefs tied about their heads, and that each of them had a machet [cutlass] and pistol in their hands.'

The portraits found in Captain Johnson's *A General History* are not reliable evidence of pirate appearance because they were not done from life and changed over time. Here, in an illustration from the original 1724 edition, Blackbeard is depicted in a fur cap and wearing a single baldric. In a later edition he appears wearing a hat, with his six pistols attached to his cartridge-box sling.

Anne Bonny and Mary Read, as depicted in the original 1724 edition of *A General History*, wearing a version of contemporary sailors' clothing.

Since in those days jackets, and especially trousers, were frequently worn by sailors, and the attack took place at sea, it seems likely that Read and Bonny were dressed as seamen. They probably looked much the same as their male pirate comrades in the raid because the witness remarked that what distinguished the two women from their companions was 'the largeness of their breasts'. It could be that pirates were so seldom described by those who saw them simply because they looked much the same as other sailors. For these reasons, one can come closest to understanding pirate dress by studying common seamen's clothing of the period, concentrating on British and American examples, since men of those nations formed the majority of pirate crews.

We get our clearest idea of the range of garments used by seamen of this era from period images and documents, including paintings, illustrations from

**B** **THE PIRATE, 1690–1725**

If a modern-day movie pirate or pirate re-enactor were somehow transported back to the Golden Age of Piracy, he would no doubt draw some very curious looks. Today's ideas of 'pirate dress' – including headscarves, hoop earrings and long, dangling sashes – are myths inspired by authors and illustrators who needed to create a recognizable pirate archetype in order to tell their stories. Real pirates were sailors who had turned outlaw and there simply is no evidence that they ever dressed as anything other than seamen. But even our ideas of late-17th- and early 18th-century seamen are obscured by legend. Here is how they actually dressed, in practical clothing of wool, linen and fustian. They wore their hair relatively short and favoured caps and small, narrow-brimmed hats rather than full-sized tricornes when at sea.

Around our picture we see a variety of sailor headgear, starting with a leather cap covered with red wool (**1**), a knitted Monmouth cap (**2**), a cloth cap trimmed with fur (**3**) and a low-crowned hat with a narrow brim (**4**). Seamen of the era wore many garments that were the same as those worn by working-class men ashore, including shirts with narrow band collars and cuffs (**5**) and sleeved waistcoats and jackets (**6**). Long woollen smocks known as 'sea gowns' (**7**) and knitted gloves or mittens (**8**) helped keep out the cold whilst on watch. Round-toed shoes with small buckles (**9**) were worn with stockings held up by tied garters (**10**). Finally, in addition to regular breeches, seamen wore wide-legged 'petticoat breeches' (**11**) as well as trousers (**12**) reaching to ankle length or higher.

books and pamphlets, heraldry (sailors sometimes appear as supporters for coats of arms), descriptions, inventories, wills and especially the 'slop-clothing' contracts the British Admiralty made with merchants for standardized clothing to be sold to ships' crews. In an era long before uniforms were issued to naval ratings, there is nothing we know of in their dress to distinguish military from civilian sailors.

Surviving examples of sailors' clothing include Russian Tsar Peter I's English and Dutch sailor clothes, garments from archaeological sites, including Scottish and Irish 'bog burials', and also shipwrecks. Archaeologists have noted, however, that there is almost nothing to distinguish pirate sites from those of other seamen of the era.

Seamen's – and thus pirates' – clothing in the late 17th and early 18th centuries was practical, durable and much like that of working-class landsmen. If anything, pirates were likely to be better supplied with clothing than other seamen of the day. It is likely that any seamen considering a career change would want to see a pirate crew dressed at least as well as themselves, if not better, before joining them. In fact, the articles of agreement under which Roberts and his men sailed guaranteed every man 'a shift of clothing' out of the booty of each ship they took. Some other captains offered the first men to board a prize the pick of the captured clothes. Though these would have included the wardrobes of officers and any gentlemen passengers, a pirate at sea would likely prefer his choice of the crew's clothes for his own use because they were better suited to his work. From inventories of captured pirates' belongings, it appears that finer garments, both men's and women's, were mostly kept for sale ashore. Pirates relied on colonial towns and even cities as markets for their booty, and like other sailors they could purchase new and used clothing at the local shops before returning to sea. Finally, as seamen, most pirates would be accustomed to making and mending their own clothes.

We must not present too tidy a picture of the pirate's personal appearance. Many were undisciplined, profligate and often drunk even on cruises. But the ragged vagabond of fiction, dressed in colourfully tattered and exotic garments, must be compared with eyewitness descriptions such as this one of two Dutch pirates in Madagascar in 1716: '[One] was dressed in a short coat with broad, plate buttons, and other things agreeable, but without shoes or stockings. In his sash was stuck a brace of pistols, and he had one in his right hand. The other man was dressed in an English manner, with two pistols in his sash and one in his hand, like his companion.'

Clothes of hard-wearing linen and wool were the most practical for life at sea. From various sources we know that the woollens sailors favoured included broadcloth, noted for the quality of its finish and colour; kersey, good at keeping out wet and cold; shag, a sturdy cloth that was something like a coarse velvet; Welsh plains, resembling flannel; and 'cotton', an inexpensive woollen cloth that got its name from its fuzzy surface. Fabrics made of actual cotton fibre were at that time expensive imports, though fustian, which wove together cotton and linen yarns, was used for cheap clothing.

A rather more racy depiction of Anne Bonny and Mary Read, from the 1725 Dutch edition of *A General History*. Like the earlier illustrations of these women, their appearance was based on nothing more than the artist's imagination.

Pirates and other seamen were not necessarily drab in appearance. Woollens seen in period paintings and fabric sample books came in light and dark blue, plum, olive, crimson and red as well as all shades of tan, brown and grey. The slops contracts include quite a bit of red fabric, perhaps reflecting the seamen's preference. There are even 'Strip'd Shagg' breeches, which may have been red and black, based on another English source from 1703. Linen does not hold dye as well as wool, but in pictures and documents related to seamen linen is seldom plain but is often dyed blue or woven with blue or red checks or stripes. Buttonhole stitching for naval slops clothing usually matched the colour of the buttons rather than the garment.

Sailors chose materials for some articles of dress because they held up well in the wet conditions aboard ship. Leather was blackened whenever possible and buckles and other metal fittings were most often made of brass, not iron. Buttons could also be brass, as well as tin, bone, horn, thread and fabric-covered disks.

Moving from the general to the particular, seamen wore various kinds of headgear. Knitted caps were very popular as well as practical, since they were warm and stayed on the head even in high winds. They appear in inventories, pictures and the Royal Navy slops contracts. Naval seamen, and probably also civilians, wore leather caps, some covered with woollen cloth, though we know little about these. They may have resembled the round-crowned jockey caps with upturned peaks popular with soldiers, hunters and Thames boatmen, among others. Seamen are often shown wearing fur-trimmed cloth caps, and Blackbeard himself is described in *A General History* as wearing one of these. There is no evidence for the use of tricorne hats during the Golden Age of Piracy by sailors at sea. Perhaps a full-sized tricorne is just not practical aboard a sailing vessel, where the jutting front point of the hat could block a man's view of the rigging overhead and low hatch covers and beams below deck, or could be caught by the wind in a gale. When some sailors finally began wearing tricornes in the 1730s, they were very small and usually worn backwards, which allows a clear view above. From pictorial and written evidence, it is clear that the seaman's favourite hat from the late 17th century right into the 19th was what buccaneer William Dampier called 'a little cropt hat' – small, round-crowned and with a narrow brim.

There simply is no evidence that what is now called a 'pirate-style' headscarf was ever a common or singularly nautical head covering, much less one distinctive to pirates. Our only example of its use by pirates comes from that description given above, when on at least that occasion Mary Read and Anne Bonny wore 'handkerchiefs tied about their heads'. But even when images of seamen wearing headscarves finally do appear towards the end of the 18th century, they are usually just temporary sweatbands tied *around* the head just as the Read and Bonny description suggests. Sometimes they cover the head, but in either case they are most often knotted on the forehead rather than at the back of the neck. The belief that headscarves were commonly worn by pirates can be traced to 19th- and 20th-century illustrators and writers, as will be shown below.

The rest of the sailor's wardrobe was simple enough, and most of his garments had their parallels ashore. They wore the common shirts of the era, which pulled on over the head and usually had narrow band collars and cuffs. Shirts found in the slops contracts include 'blew and white chequer'd Linnen' as well as entirely blue ones. From the hips down they wore garments variously

Small round hats and knitted caps were the most popular headgear for sailors from the late 17th through to the early 19th century. Headscarves (seen on the right) were far less common and were frequently tied on the forehead, as seen here in Thomas Rowlandson's 1798 cartoon celebrating the battle of the Nile.

This Encouraged, *England* muſt Flouriſh.

Pirates looked quite unlike our popular image, dressing much the same as other British sailors. Here, in a cartouche entitled *England's Safety*, we see two British seamen in fur caps and checked petticoat breeches from 1693.

classified as breeches, petticoat breeches, slops or trousers. All began with a similar waistband and some kind of fly closure. The real difference seems to be in the legs. Breeches usually fastened at the knees with buttons or tape ties but some were simply hemmed at the bottom and left open. Petticoat breeches had wide and open legs and sometimes artists of the period show them worn over breeches or drawers, leaving open the question of whether they were ever used just by themselves. Trousers varied in length from mid-shin to above the ankles. 'Slops' is sometimes used to mean petticoat breeches but also loose trousers reaching below the knees. All of these leg coverings could be made of wool, linen (including canvas) or fustian, while the woollen as well as linen breeches of the slops contracts were lined with linen. Waistcoats and jackets were roughly hip-length, sleeved and collarless. But while the waistcoats of the slops contracts were made of linen or wool, only one kind of jacket is mentioned, and it is of wool. In fact, it is of 'shrunck' (i.e. boiled) kersey and lined with wool 'cotton', which means that it would not only be warm but also water-resistant. Finally, sashes seldom appear on British and American sailors of this era, though Spanish and French seamen used them. But wherever used, they were small, neat affairs used to keep jackets closed or to support weapons, not the long, flowing sort found in fiction.

Aboard ship, sailors often went barefoot, but if not they wore shoes. Britain's navy supplied its men with rugged shoes, described as made of 'neat's leather' (cowhide), and as being 'waxed', 'double-soled' (made with a welt of leather sewn between the sole and upper to keep out water) and with rounded toes. Rounded toes, along with low heels and short tongues were common features of working men's shoes of the era. These have been found aboard shipwrecks, but so have shoes with the more fashionable squared toes and high heels, indicating perhaps a difference in footwear between officers and men. In the case of pirates, outfitting themselves from their prizes, it may be that both styles were seen. Royal Navy slops contracts include brass shoe buckles with iron tongues. Unlike the popular image of pirates, shoe buckles of the era were quite small, approximately 2.5cm by 1.25cm. Latchets (laces) could be used in place of buckles.

There is little written or pictorial evidence in this era for foul-weather gear to protect seamen against extremes of cold or wet, but of course it must have existed. Since storage space was scarce, it could be that most of this gear belonged to the ship and was issued to men for the duration of their watch. This could explain why the only foul-weather clothing mentioned in the Royal Navy slops contracts is 'Kersey gowns', in 1690. Elsewhere, we find the names 'sea gown' and 'watch gown'. Dampier used his 'sea gown' as a covering when sleeping ashore, which suggests that it was large, and a few period images show seamen wearing knee-length smocks. Perhaps these were similar to a knee-length woollen shirt found in a bog burial at Arnish Moor, in Scotland, that was worn beneath the much shorter jacket found on the same body. Sailors might also have worn their sea gowns beneath their thick jackets, and could add to this lined woollen breeches, a woollen waistcoat, stockings, gloves or mittens and a knitted wool cap when they needed to keep warm. All are mentioned in contemporary records. To keep dry, sailors have long painted the ship's pine tar on canvas clothing, perhaps earning British sailors the nickname of 'tars', which appears as early as 1676. Water-resistant leather sea boots appear in early 18th-century images of Spanish and French sailors, and were likely used by other mariners, including pirates. Since these were only needed in the worst weather, and seldom appear in personal inventories, perhaps these too were kept in limited numbers aboard ship and used by whoever was standing watch. Though the wearing of horsemen's boots by pirates and other seafarers is part of the mythical pirate 'look', it is completely unsupported by either research or reason.

By showing pirate captains dressed as gentlemen and their crews clothed as common seamen, *A General History* presented to its audience a view of pirate society they both understood and expected – one where someone's rank and class was easily distinguished by their clothing. And though this convention has lasted in the popular imagination right down from the story of Captain Hook to today, it is unlikely that this was actually the case with pirates. Against the description of Bartholomew Roberts' battle dress of crimson damask found in *A General History*, we have from the same source Roberts' own articles, which as captain only allowed him two shares of the value of a prize compared with one share each for the lowest-ranking members of the crew. This was probably typical, since similar divisions are

When *Treasure Island* was presented on stage in New York City in 1911 the mythical pirate costume was already accepted as fact. Motion pictures were soon to establish this image around the world.

found in other pirate articles. Thus captains were generally no more than twice as rich as their crewmen, and as such not likely to dress very much better. The fiercely egalitarian society of a pirate ship may not have encouraged the display of rank through dress, and in any case officers had no special claim to rich clothing that might form part of the plunder. In 1716 three pirate commanders on the West African coast who took some fine coats from the captain of a captured merchant ship were scolded by their crews, who feared that if they were not challenged these officers would in future 'take whatever they liked for themselves'. The coats were confiscated and sold at the mast.

## The pirate of popular imagination

Since the dress of real pirates of this period, both of officers and men, was so different from the popular image now accepted around the world, we must ask where this image came from. The answer, in a word, is 'marketing'. As early as the first edition of *A General History*, pirates were presented to the public in clothing and descriptions that seem intended to make them appear as colourful as their often-exaggerated reputations. This was and remains a problem.

A pirate was just an outlaw sailor, but in order to sell books and later plays, ballets, operettas, movies, toys, festivals and a host of other products to the public, it is necessary to make pirates instantly recognizable and exciting – one has to sell the *fantasy* of pirates. This meant creating an image that the public could recognize instantly as a pirate and not mistake for an honest sailor.

*A General History* at least showed pirate crewmen dressed as common seamen of the day, and the officers as merely over-dressed. But by the beginning of the 19th century the image of pirates had long since ceased to be in any way historical. The dress of pirate captains was especially exaggerated by illustrators and theatrical costumiers out of any relationship to reality, drawing on a wealth of different sources to mix such elements as Napoleonic-era bicorn hats or broad-brimmed sombreros with tights, fringed petticoats, doublets, striped jerseys, musketeer or heavy-cavalry boots, scimitars and fierce whiskers and mustachios. These pirates frequently wore the skull-and-crossbones on hats, aprons and other garments as if it were a corporate logo. This fantastic type of pirate hero was justly satirized in the costumes for the original production of Gilbert and Sullivan's operetta *The Pirates of Penzance* (1879). Robert Louis Stevenson's novel *Treasure Island* (first serialized 1881–82) tried to reclaim the historical pirate by giving him a much more realistic appearance. The plot of the book hinges on the fact that there was no difference between the dress of honest and dishonest seamen, which allows the pirate Long John Silver to con Squire Trelawney into hiring him and his old shipmates for the treasure-hunting expedition.

But it was the American author and illustrator Howard Pyle (1853–1911) who invented our modern ideas of pirate dress, by blending fantasy with the appearance of reality through his now-classic stories and pictures. Beginning in 1887, Pyle modified the dress first of buccaneers and then of pirates by adding elements of Spanish folk costume, especially headscarves knotted behind the head, large hoop earrings and broad, trailing sashes. These are the same clothing elements we associate with Gypsies – Spain being the common connection. For it was the Spanish Main where buccaneers and pirates roamed in Pyle's lively imagination. Though Pyle was widely recognized in his day as a historical illustrator, his use of Spanish elements was not based on research – there is no evidence to support them – but on the same need illustrators have always felt to make buccaneers and pirates colourful and instantly recognizable to their audiences. In fact, headscarves, hoop earrings and long sashes were not even part of 17th- and 18th-century Spanish or Spanish-American folk costume, though they were in Pyle's own day. Pyle was also mistaken in his notions of early 18th-century sailor dress, but his combination of tricorne hats, long queues, boots and big square buckles with headscarves, earrings and sashes was a stroke of creative genius that resulted in a very believable and seductive archetype. It is also a durable one. Though modified by the addition of the skull-and-crossbones, striped jerseys, eye patches, prosthetic hooks and even mascara and dreadlocks, Pyle's archetypal pirates remain at the core of an image that has spread through film and other popular media around the world.

The American illustrator Howard Pyle (1853–1911) created the archetypal pirate we all know today. Pyle's pirates typically wear large tricorne hats, headscarves, hoop earrings and long, flowing sashes – none of which appear in the historical record for either sailors or pirates of the Golden Age of Piracy.

Contemporary Spanish folk costume seen in an American magazine illustration from the late 19th century. Howard Pyle created his pirates by combining such costume with what he believed (incorrectly) was typical sailor clothing of the early 18th century.

# A PIRATE'S LIFE

Piracy was not something to be taken lightly. Most new pirates – volunteers or otherwise – would have known that their life expectancy was low. When Bartholomew Roberts' crew were tried at Cape Coast Castle in West Africa in 1722 the authorities described a handful of them 'old standers and notorious offenders'. In other words, these were men who had been pirates longer than the rest, even though the most experienced had only become pirates less than four years before. The majority had been pirates for less than two years, which appears to be the typical lifespan of a seaman who 'followed the black flag'.

This cold fact encouraged pirates to live for the moment, and to embrace a different style of living from anything they had experienced before. This lack of longevity should have deterred sailors from joining a pirate crew, but this was balanced with a sense of freedom that proved highly attractive to pirate recruits. During this period many seamen suffered from low wages, harsh discipline, hard unremitting labour, damp and crowded living quarters, bad or insufficient food and a repressive regimen of injustice and oppression. By joining a pirate crew they were able to improve their lot with a share of plunder, better victuals, a plentiful supply of alcohol and the freedom to elect officers and to have a say in their own collective future.

Before becoming a pirate, there was the ever-present risk of injury or death through accidents or drowning. These remained part of the pirate's lot, but where before the injured were seen as an extra mouth to feed, and were put ashore at the next port, on a pirate ship they would be cared for, or at least guaranteed their fair share of the spoils. There was also a heightened sense of companionship, as their new shipmates all shared the same poor life

Pirates had to be seamen first and outlaws second. The daily routine of shipboard duties, not plundering or swashbuckling, was the common reality of pirate life. In this 19th-century illustration the pirate Henry Avery and his crew are loading a plundered cargo onto their own vessel.

Pirates, too, including Edward Low pictured here, were subject to the will of the weather, sometimes at its most violent. Pirate shipwrecks have revealed important information about the daily lives of these sea rovers.

expectancy, and a desire to make the most of the present. Bartholomew Roberts is supposed to have said to a prisoner that a pirate's life had given him 'plenty and satiety, pleasure and ease, liberty and power... No, a merry life and a short one shall be my motto.'

This being said, life on board a pirate ship was not as egalitarian as some would have us believe. The evidence supplied by the court records of pirate trials shows us that a hierarchy existed, and that the 'liberty and power' espoused by Roberts was not necessarily enjoyed in equal measure on board a pirate ship.

New recruits had to demonstrate a commitment to their new life and to their shipmates. They had to prove themselves, to show their effectiveness in action, before they were accepted as full members of the pirate crew. According to Captain Johnson, the pirate captain Thomas Cocklyn reportedly beat new recruits, while Israel Hynde, the boatswain on Bartholomew Roberts' ship, 'was always swearing and cursing at the new pirates'. On some ships new recruits were excluded from the normally democratic discussions that formed a major part of pirate decision-making, and were not permitted to go aboard prizes, until their allegiance had been proven. However, once they became integrated into the crew they enjoyed a level of freedom they had never experienced at sea, and a level of companionship that was heightened by the shared sense of belonging to a special pirate society.

This social order might have appeared anarchic to outsiders such as captured ship captains or seamen, but it was designed by the pirates themselves to suit their own needs. There was a structure that governed pirate life, even though it flew in the face of the established order of the period. It created a rough-and-ready form of egalitarianism, where no man on board – not even the captain – was raised above the rest, and where authority was held collectively, or by officers who could be elected or deposed by the collective will of the crew. The system had its roots in the buccaneering charters of the previous century, whose democratic approach had a lasting impact on the privateersmen of Jamaica, who were their natural successors.

In 1713, when the former privateer Hornigold established a pirate haven on New Providence, there were still a few 'old hands' who remembered the old system and how it worked. It made perfect sense to base the structure of a pirate ship along these old egalitarian lines, as they reflected a halcyon period when seamen weren't oppressed by work, wages and conditions, but had a say in their own affairs. While some historians have claimed great things of these pirates, claiming that they were embarking on a social revolution and turning the old order on its head, the likelihood is that the men themselves simply wanted a system where they could control their own fate during the few short months or years they remained at large.

This was one reason why pirates were demonised by the authorities, and described as 'the common enemies of mankind'. It wasn't just their crimes that were a danger – their egalitarian approach to life might lead to unrest amongst merchant seamen and therefore threaten the transatlantic shipping business, a source of great wealth to Britain and the other maritime powers. Conversely, when word of their democratic principles leaked out, pirates were admired by working sailors, who envied the freedom these criminals enjoyed. For those without commitments or responsibilities back home, this system of self-determination must have seemed extremely attractive, and would certainly influence the decision of seamen to join a pirate crew if their ship was captured.

Pirates operated under two forms of authority, one imposed through written 'articles' (effectively a pirate code of conduct) and the other by the collective will of the crew. The crew could vote on just about every aspect of their lives, including where to sail, who to attack, whether to spare prisoners or their vessels, what punishments to inflict on those who flouted the articles, or who would hold positions of authority, from the captain and quartermaster to the boatswain's mate. The written articles dealt with the authority of

### THE PIRATE CAPTAIN

Ever since the imagined portraits were published in the first edition of *A General History*, the general public has come to believe that pirate captains and other officers dressed much better than their men – perhaps even like gentlemen in laced coats and plumed hats. But there is almost no evidence to support this notion, and many reasons to believe that, at best, pirate officers only dressed somewhat better than their men and were very often indistinguishable from them. On the other hand, officers could wear the longer coats and sleeved waistcoats that their men would find inconvenient in their work, and their larger shares of booty would allow them to acquire, sometimes by purchase, some of the finer clothes that fell to the pirates through plunder.

Our pirate captain has pulled on over his everyday clothing some of his share of a successful raid, consisting of a gentleman's plumed hat, a curled wig and a fine coat. Appearing around him (not to scale) are the kinds of garments known to have been favoured by maritime officers and petty officers of the day: a cloth cap trimmed with fine fur (**1**), a sleeved waistcoat of moderate length (**2**), well-made breeches (**3**), shoes of a fashionable style (**4**), a gentleman's short sash (**5**), which was usually worn around the coat and knotted in front, and a knee-length sleeved waistcoat with slashed and buttoned cuffs (**6**).

1

2

3

4

5

6

G. Rava '11

officers, the distribution of plunder, food or drink and the imposition of rules to aid the good governance of the pirate vessel. An example of these articles survives, having been captured on board Bartholomew Roberts' flagship by the crew of HMS *Swallow* in February 1722. They were published by Captain Johnson two years later in his *General History*.

The combination of written articles and governance by the majority produced circumstances that were alien to most prisoners who witnessed pirate crews in operation. For a start, a pirate captain only had authority over his crew when pursuing or attacking a prize, or when evading an enemy. Otherwise his actions were governed by the decision of the majority. There are cases of a captain wanting to spare captured vessels, but being overruled by the crew, who elected to set them on fire. Others, such as Charles Vane, were deposed from office for making decisions that didn't meet with the approval of their shipmates. To the pirates, this was understandable. They had recently escaped from one form of authoritarian system and they had no wish to replace it with one of their own.

The seaman Barnaby Slush described this relationship in 1709, having experienced life amongst the Jamaican privateers and former buccaneers:

> Pyrates and Buccaneers are princes to [merchant seamen], for there as none are exempt from the general toil and danger. So, if their Chief have a supream share beyond his comrades, 'tis because he's always the leading man in e'ry daring enterprize; And yet, as bold as he is in all other attempts, he dares not offer to infringe the common laws of equity, but every associate has his due quota … thus these hostes humani generis as great robbers, as they are to all besides, are precisely just among themselves, without which they could no more subsist than a structure without a foundation.

The role of quartermaster was intended as a check on the authority of the captain, but it was also key to the running of the ship because he supervised the division of plunder. When Captain William Snelgrave was captured by pirates off the West African coast in 1719 he was able to describe the quartermaster's role: 'He has the general inspection of all affairs, and often controuls the Captain's orders. This person is also to be the first man in boarding any ship they shall attack; or go in the boat in any desperate enterprize.' Captain Johnson's description was more revealing: 'We may say the Quarter-master is an humble imitation of the Roman tribune of the people – he speaks for, and looks after the interest of the crew.' In other words, he held a position of trust and power amongst the crew, even though he remained one of them.

He dispensed food and drink as equitably as possible, particularly if the crew were on short rations because of a lack of provisions, and organized the teams who would form boarding parties to take control of a prize. This was an important perk, as the men who first came aboard a captured vessel were allowed certain privileges, such as the first selection of captured clothing or drink. The rest of the plunder was held in a common pool, having been selected by the quartermaster, and sometimes the goods were even recorded in a ledger. He was responsible for looking after these goods, and for their division when the time came.

While some of this plunder might be money or valuable commodities such as gold dust or jewels, the rest would have been a more mundane collection of goods, which were loaded into the hold of the pirate ship for sale or division at a later date. If the captured ship contained a cargo of wine or spirits, it was more usual for this to be brought over to the pirate vessel, and the pirates would try their best to drink their way through it. Taking some of this plunder without the consent of the majority of the crew was seen as a particularly serious offence. In 1719, when Howell Davis and two other pirate officers went ashore in Sierra Leone in search of local women, they dressed themselves in captured finery from the common store. William Snelgrave described how the crew resented this, and ordered Davis and his

Though jealous of their own freedom, pirates were more likely to sell a captured slave than to recruit him into their crews. Here, an imagined portrait of a suspiciously well-dressed Henry Avery depicts him as a grandee, accompanied by an African servant.

companions to return the clothing. As Snelgrave put it: 'If they suffered such things, the Captains would for the future assume a power, to take whatever they liked for themselves.'

Snelgrave also noted that this egalitarian spirit manifested itself in other unusual ways. The crew of the vessel slept wherever they liked, including in any cabins, and the captain and his officers had to sleep wherever they could. This prevented any of them from assuming the trappings that usually went with their position on board other ships, and reminded them that they were elected and owed their position to their shipmates. Of course, some captains managed to exert their authority regardless of these restrictions, either through repeated success (Roberts), fear and intimidation (Blackbeard) or by spearheading a common cause, such as revenge (Bonnet).

While observers like Snelgrave give us an idea of how a pirate crew organized its affairs, they remained irritatingly quiet on some key matters. How did they organize watches? Did the seamen take orders from the more experienced foremast men and boatswains? Were the crew fed at set times, as on board a merchant vessel, or was the system more fluid? It would seem sensible to infer that because Snelgrave and others never mentioned these matters the system used by the pirates was similar to that which the observers were used to. In other words, pirates stood watches, formed teams to operate the sails or man the guns, and took a part in the everyday maintenance and operation of the ship, just like they would have done on board a merchantman. The difference, of course, was that they had a say in how these watches were organized, and that duties were probably shared far more equitably than would have been the case on board a more conventional sailing ship.

One key area where these observers noticed a difference between pirate and merchant crews was in self-indulgence. While on a merchant ship poor rations and a lack of spirits were commonplace; on board a pirate ship both were literally there for the taking. Prizes carrying alcohol or with large stocks of food on board were welcomed, as they replenished the stocks of both key provisions. Men like Snelgrave commented on the heavy drinking, and how decisions were often reached by the crew 'over a large bowl of [rum] punch'.

**D** **LIFE AT SEA**

'Kennelling like hounds on the deck' was how one captain likened the accommodation of pirates at sea. Pirate crews were much larger than those in the merchant service, and men were crowded together aboard their vessels, living wherever they could. It only required a fraction of these crews to operate the vessel, so idleness was a problem. Add to this the heat of the tropics, the liberal use of alcohol and the touchy pride of men who jealously defended the equality they gained by joining the democracy of pirates, and one can easily see how difficult maintaining discipline could be.

Pirate society was governed by the articles crewmen and officers signed on joining, which were an attempt to impose a legal system all could agree to. A ban on gambling at sea was a common rule among pirates, so common indeed that it was probably not widely observed by men who would lurk about the ship through long days and nights with little else to do. Drinking was not prohibited, but the articles often required that it be done on deck for fear of fire breaking out below or that the men could not be roused out in an emergency to defend or work the ship. Pirate officers were elected and could just as easily be deposed by the vote of the crew they commanded, so even the word 'commanded' might not be quite accurate. After all, unlike the merchant and naval services, where the arms chest was kept safely locked away to prevent mutinies, another common pirate article required that every man keep his weapons cleaned and ready to hand for immediate use.

The right to food and drink was enshrined in the first clause of Roberts' articles, but this unlimited access brought its own problems. Snelgrave described the scene when his captors seized a cargo of wine and spirits:

> They hoisted upon deck a great many half-hogsheads of claret, and French brandy; knocked their heads out, and dipped cans and bowls into them to drink out of. And in their wantonness threw full buckets of each sort upon one another. As soon as they had emptied what was on the deck, they hoisted up more: and in the evening washed the decks with what remained in the casks. As to bottled liquor of many sorts, they made such havoc of it, that in a few days they had not one bottle left: For they would not give themselves the trouble of drawing the cork out, but nicked the bottles, as they called it, that is, struck their necks off with a cutlace; by which means one in three was generally broke: Neither was there any cask-liquor left in a short time, but a little brandy. As to eatables, such as cheeses, butter, sugar, and many other things, they were as soon gone. For the Pirates being all in a drunken fit, which held as long as the liquor lasted, no care was taken by any one to prevent this destruction.

Naturally, these bacchanalian scenes were detrimental to efficiency. 'Calico Jack' Rackam's crew were captured by a pirate hunter in November 1720 as they lay at anchor off the western tip of Jamaica, having spent the night drinking with local turtle fishermen. Observers tell of pirates and their prizes lying next to each other for days, as the drunken pirates were unable to hoist a sail. Even a charismatic pirate leader such as Blackbeard was unable to completely control his crew during times like these, and consequently pirate crews were occasionally taken by surprise, as happened to Rackam, Bonnet, Roberts and even Blackbeard himself.

Pirates certainly knew how to enjoy themselves, with little thought for what tomorrow might bring. However, Snelgrave was less impressed by what he saw as lack of moral virtue: 'The execrable oaths and blasphemies I heard among the ship's company, shocked me to such a degree, that in Hell its self I thought there could not be worse; for though many seafaring men are given to swearing and taking God's name in vain, yet I could not have imagined, human nature could ever so far degenerate, as to talk in the manner those abandoned Wretches did.' With this reputation for freedom, hard drinking and a disregard for conventional morals, it is little wonder that young, impressionable seamen welcomed the opportunity to join a pirate crew, even though they knew the risks. In exchange for all that freedom, they were also effectively signing their own death warrant.

## VIOLENCE

Pirates in general saw no profit in battle. To begin with, it was dangerous. If not killed outright, a pirate could be badly wounded, which might become worse because of infection and crude surgical practices. Combat could also damage or even sink a prize, so pirates usually tried to use intimidation up until the last possible moment, hoping that the other vessel would surrender. When all else failed, however, they could fight with desperate determination. After all, whether through death in battle or by hanging if captured, they were fighting for their lives.

Pirate vessels often lurked in hidden bays and estuaries or behind low islands, waiting for their prey. From a high mast a lookout could scan the horizon for many miles. When a likely victim was spotted the pirates would ease their vessels out into open water and follow, sometimes shadowing the other ship for hours or even days. The captain, usually assisted by the more-experienced quartermaster, would study the prospective prize through spyglasses to try and determine its nationality, destination, cargo and much else before considering an attack. Lambs might be disguised as wolves – for lightly armed merchantmen could have false gun ports painted along their sides. But they could also be wolves in fact, a comparatively rare man-of-war, which the pirates would want very much to avoid. A decision as important as this was seldom left to the elected officers; a vote had to be taken that included all the shareholders in the venture – that is, both officers and crew. Should the measure pass, subsequent events unfolded rapidly.

If the targeted merchantman had not spotted the pirates before this, they soon did. A shot would cross their bow as one or more vessels sailed straight at them, pirate flags flying, which were usually black banners bearing grim devices.

Pirate tactics generally depended on the size and number of both the attackers and the victims. The majority of pirates used small, fast vessels that could outrun and outmanoeuvre their prey. These could also be used in consort with larger craft, even ships, which by nautical tradition must carry three masts. In either case, pirates relied on having more guns and larger crews than merchantmen usually carried. Large crews were needed not only for boarding but to work all of the guns. Two pirate vessels with a total of fifty guns between them could stand up to anything afloat except a naval man-of-war.

Though not necessarily intending violence, the pirate crew would prepare for battle. Guns were loaded and run out, men not already on deck joined their fellows and every man was heavily armed. Unlike merchantmen and

Smaller, single-masted vessels, such as the sloop, were used both by pirates and by their pursuers. This colonial American sloop of the 1720s is pictured off Boston Light.

even men-of-war, weapons aboard a pirate vessel were not kept locked away in chests under the control of the captain or quartermaster. According to most pirate articles, each man was expected to keep his own arms cleaned and ready for use. Purchased privately or acquired through plunder, not only English but French, Dutch and Spanish weapons were available to pirates, varying greatly in make, quality and calibre.

Muskets were useful for sniping at enemy crews, while the shorter blunderbusses and musketoons were shock weapons, fired on the point of boarding. Most pirates carried one or more pistols into action. To minimize rust, as much of the metal of these weapons as possible was brass, even including barrels on some blunderbusses and pistols.

When fighting hand-to-hand on crowded decks, seamen preferred short weapons. Cutlasses of this period had blades of 28in. (71cm) or less, and were slightly curved. These were primarily used for chopping and slashing,

 **WEAPONRY**

In addition to his nautical skills, a pirate needed to be able to fight. Here are the tools of his trade (not shown to scale). A pirate vessel was usually better supplied with guns (**1**) than a merchant vessel and the guns were better manned. Many pirates were former naval seamen who brought with them their valuable knowledge of gunnery. On a moving vessel, guns had to be tied down to keep them from rolling about crushing people and things. The rope tackle was also used to move the gun into position after the recoil of firing. The gun's implements (**2**) were similar to those used on land, with the powder ladle made of bronze or wood to avoid sparks and the rammer and sponge often mounted on a flexible rope to assist loading and cleaning the gun in tight quarters. Swivel guns (**3**) were smaller and served to repel boarders or were mounted on boats. Grenadoes (**4**) were made of cast iron or improvised from bottles, and loaded with gunpowder and lit with wooden fuses. Valuable pistols (**5**) could easily be lost overboard or dropped in an attack, so many pirates attached them to their persons with cloth slings around their necks or torsos (**6**). Muskets were for longer-range sniping. Shown here is a Royal Navy dog-lock musket completely lacquered in black to prevent rust (**7**). Shorter blunderbusses and musketoons (**8**) were used, like pistols, for boarding or in close fighting. In a crowded skirmish aboard a ship, cutlasses (**9**), boarding axes (**10**) and pikes (**11**) were favoured. Men needed almost no training to be effective with these. Sailors' knives (**12**) were primarily tools, and used only as a last resort in battle.

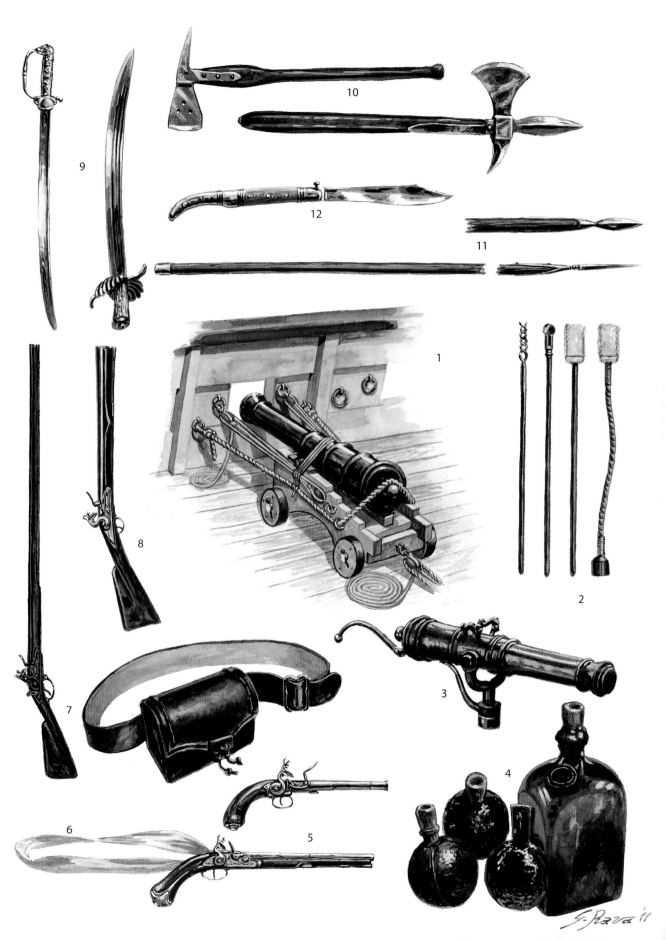

and required no great skill in fencing to be effective. The blades were fitted with guards of either cast brass or wrought iron. Boarding axes were as useful for clearing fallen rigging as splitting heads. Typical axes had a blade on one side and a spike on the other. There is some evidence for the British adding a spear tip at the top, though none of these seem to have survived. Boarding pikes were simply short spears with spike or leaf-shaped blades, and wooden shafts. Except in extreme circumstances, knives were not combat weapons and were more useful for brawls or murder.

It is not always clear how pirates carried their arms and ammunition. *A General History* describes both Bartholomew Roberts and Blackbeard with several pairs of pistols on slings across their bodies. A pistol with a linen sling tied to its grip was found in the 1717 wreck of the pirate ship *Whydah*, and seems to have fulfilled the same purpose. Unlike naval and merchant cutlasses, which were stored in chests, pirates probably kept theirs in scabbards hung from either shoulder or waist belts, while blackened leather and brass fittings would be useful in resisting damp at sea. At the beginning of the Golden Age of Piracy two methods of carrying small-arms ammunition were in use. On the wreck of a ship that was carrying Massachusetts militia men when it sank in 1690, archaeologists found a late form of 'apostle' belt (powder flasks and a bag containing balls and wadding all attached to a bandolier) as well as a cartridge box. Cartridges were the

Pirates and other seamen of the day favoured the short cutlass for combat, either with a wrought-iron guard, such as the one shown here, or a lighter and more ornamental guard of cast brass. This engraving shows the French buccaneer L'Olonais, from Exquemelin's *Buccaneers of America*, published in Amsterdam in 1678.

The larger brigantine, with crews of about 100 men, was often accompanied by one or more smaller vessels to form pirate flotillas capable of taking on more ambitious targets.

This French slave ship of around 1715 is similar to *La Concorde*, the vessel captured by Blackbeard in late 1717 and converted into the pirate flagship *Queen Anne's Revenge*.

next stage in the evolution of ammunition, conveniently combining powder, wadding and balls into single packets. But the 1717 wreck of the pirate ship *Whydah* yielded only cartridge boxes and no apostles, suggesting that the transition to the new ammunition was complete. These boxes were probably carried on waist belts. Shoulder-slung cartridge boxes as well as priming flasks are also likely, but so far no examples of them have been found.

Now that the men were armed the pirate officers would 'spirit up' the crew, encouraging them to drink heartily both to give them 'Dutch courage' and to dull the pain of wounds in battle. Not that the crew needed much encouragement.

At this point, though, the pirates still tried to avoid direct attack. The merchant vessel was hailed; its captain ordered to put off in a boat and come aboard. Often the sight of the pirate ship's guns and a hundred or more drunken and armed brigands was very persuasive. If the captain did as he was ordered, the pirates not only gained an important hostage, but could also interrogate the officer about his cargo and crew. From here, the rest was plain sailing. The pirates would board in safety and plunder the ship at their leisure. If the captain refused to come aboard, then things could take a nastier turn.

Merchantmen who decided to resist capture were not entirely helpless. They did have guns, though not many and seldom as well manned as the pirates'. In the well-known case of the English vessel *Bauden*, which fought off the French pirate *Trompeuse* in 1686, the defenders cleared their decks, issued arms to the crew and set up powder chests on the poop

Pirate vessels usually advertised their intentions by flying distinctive flags. Often it was some variation of a black field with a skull-and-crossbones, but red flags and even a Union Jack with four flaming cannon balls were used. This engraving of Stede Bonnet shows the flag that was generally associated with him.

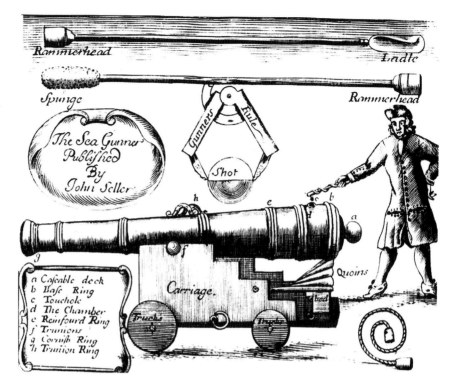

This illustration from John Seller's naval-artillery treatise *The Sea Gunner* (1691) shows a typical gun of the period, albeit a bronze one, rather than the more commonplace iron guns used on most merchant vessels. It is mounted on a four-truck carriage – note the smaller rear trucks, to help absorb the recoil of the piece.

and forecastle. The yardarms were reinforced with chains to prevent their being cut away. The decks were then spread with dried peas, a common food at sea, in hopes of making the boarders slip. There were also boards with nails driven through them, which, in the smoke of battle, might very well do some injury. The captain and crew then withdrew to the forecastle and aftercastle, heavily built cabins pierced with loopholes at either end of the deck, to await the attack.

The pirates at the same time were no doubt making their own final preparations for the coming conflict. Pirate ships usually carried musicians, including fiddlers, bagpipers, drummers and trumpeters. They entertained the men during idle hours or helped in their work by playing as the crew turned capstans or hauled on halliards and sheets. But it was probably before and during the attack that the pirates most needed their music.

 **THE PIRATE ATTACK**

Pirates seldom surprised their prey. In fact, they found that boldly announcing themselves with a shot across their enemy's bow and displaying the black flag actually worked much better. As they closed with their intended victims, pirates usually appeared on deck drunk and heavily armed. Alcohol would temporarily boost the pirates' courage and dull the pain of wounds. Frequently, they began 'vapouring', dancing about on deck to music provided by the ship's musicians, waving their weapons, shouting war cries and growling. They often added insults shouted at their prey, especially directed at the merchant captain. These antics served two purposes: intimidation and bonding. Though pirates had a reputation as eager fighters, they really had little to gain and much to lose in combat. Wounding or death for themselves and damage to or loss of a prize could all be avoided if the pirates could frighten their prey into an easy surrender. Vapouring also served to temporarily unite the pirate crew and to bolster their courage. If all this failed to bring about surrender, the pirates went into the attack. They approached combat carefully, trying to disable the merchantman rather than wound or sink her. Only as a last resort did the pirates finally board and take a prize by force.

The pirate practice of 'vapouring' may seem strange to us at first. To the music of their band, the pirates would begin dancing about the decks, waving their weapons and ringing their cutlasses together, all the time shouting and growling. But war dances have a very long history and can raise men's spirits and bond them into a unit before battle. The pirates would also loudly curse their intended victims, singling out the merchant captain for special attention. Pirate John Russel famously hailed the captain of the merchant sloop *Dolphin* off the Cape Verde Islands in 1722, shouting: 'You dog! You son of a bitch! You speckle-shirted dog! I will drub you, you dog, within an inch of your life – and that inch too!'

Even pirate captains were not above a bit of psychological warfare. Edward Teach (Blackbeard) was said to have stuck lighted fuses beneath his fur cap to further enhance his wild appearance. Bartholomew Roberts evidently sought to inspire awe and respect in his enemies when he dressed himself before his last battle in a suit of crimson damask and hung a diamond-studded cross about his neck from a golden chain.

Still trying to avoid damaging their intended prize, the pirates would open the fight with musket fire from the deck and rigging, hoping to kill or wound the captain or his crew. Their guns would fire bar or chain shot, cutting away some of their enemy's rigging. They would next attempt to cross the bow or stern of the vessel. If it was the stern, they could disable the rudder. If it was the bow, then things could get serious very quickly. First, the pirates would try and entangle the merchantman's bowsprit in their rigging. This would keep him from presenting his broadside guns to the pirates, though the pirates

already had theirs targeting him. The bowsprit also served as a boarding platform across which the pirates could scramble onto the decks of the merchantman. This was one way of boarding a victim. When Blackbeard attacked the sloop *Jane* in his last battle, he and his small crew threw grappling hooks over and hauled the vessel close.

Before boarding, pirates softened up the enemy by throwing grenadoes, either cast-iron balls or glass bottles filled with gunpowder and lit by a fuse. These exploding bombs shocked, blinded and wounded the enemy.

If the merchant crew met them on deck, then the hand-to-hand combat could be terrible. Led usually by their quartermaster, the pirates entered the fight with pistols and blunderbusses, ready to fire a single shot before being dropped so cutlasses and boarding axes could come into play. In the thick smoke the crowded decks would become a hell of clashing weapons, flashes of pistol fire, grunts, crunches and screams. Since neither side wore uniforms, it would be difficult to tell friend from foe in the fight as the conflict grew more desperate and the decks became treacherous with blood and fallen bodies. For as long as they could, the pirate band would continue to play music from the deck of their ship in order to give their comrades courage. If the conflict seemed very dire, pirate ships might at some point lower their black flags and raise red ones, signalling that no quarter would be given.

Another scenario was acted out in the case of the fight between the *Bauden* and the *Trompeuse*. Having entangled the English merchantman's bowsprit, the French pirates scaled her rigging and tried to cut away the yards, but the chains securing them prevented this. Now the pirates became

**ABOVE LEFT**

Howard Pyle's exciting illustration of Blackbeard and his crew in battle off Ocracoke Island in November 1718 captures very well the packed decks, dense smoke and close hand-to-hand duels of shipboard combat.

**ABOVE**

This imagined portrait of Bartholomew Roberts, published in 1724, is one of several examples from *A General History* showing the cartridge pouch hung in front of the wearer by a strap around the neck, which also supports several small pistols. If based on reality, this seems like a very awkward arrangement.

45

the target of small-arms fire, and several plunged wounded into the sea. Whether or not the peas or nails succeeded in tripping up the pirates, they were caught in a crossfire the minute they entered the well between the forecastle and aftercastle as shot from muskets, pistols and swivel guns cut through them. Meanwhile, the two ships continued a desultory exchange of cannon fire, which at one point exploded the merchantman's powder chest. In the end, with both pirate and merchant captains dead among many others, the pirates fled.

If pirates won the fight, the consequences could be very grim, especially for the merchant captain. Had he surrendered immediately, he might even

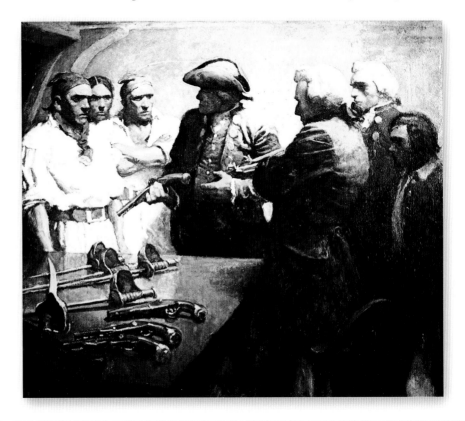

Pirates never used the kind of hand-covering brass cutlass guards shown here by the illustrator N. C. Wyeth. These were, in fact, inspired by an American Civil War cutlass in the artist's collection.

## G BATTLE

There are few better examples of the ferocity of pirates in battle than Blackbeard's last fight. Early on 22 November 1718 the pirate captain Edward Teach (Blackbeard) and his crew of 19 were surprised aboard their sloop, the *Adventure*, off Ocracoke Island, North Carolina. At the approach of two small civilian vessels and more than 60 men under the command of Royal Navy Lieutenant Robert Maynard, the outnumbered pirates fired a gun and cut their anchor cable in order to flee. A slow-motion pursuit climaxed among the sandbanks and shallows on that nearly windless morning when Blackbeard and his followers grappled and boarded the lead vessel, commanded by Lieutenant Maynard. We see here the infamous pirate engaged in a hand-to-hand duel with the naval officer, who has bent his sword against Blackbeard's cartridge box after an ill-aimed thrust at his belly. Meanwhile, Maynard's seamen, distinguished by their mostly red and grey naval slop clothing, scramble up from below decks where they had taken refuge from Blackbeard's cannon. They surprised the small band of pirates who had boarded in the belief that their fire had wiped out their pursuers. A desperate fight followed, leaving the pirates defeated and the decks awash with blood and littered with the wounded and dying. Blackbeard himself suffered perhaps five gunshot and 20 sword wounds before his head was severed. This grim trophy was hung from the bowsprit of Maynard's sloop as he returned from the battle in triumph.

have been hailed as a good fellow and treated kindly, though he would still have been robbed. But now it was only a question of when he would be killed by the pirates, not if. The rest of the crew, however, would be subjected to the usual recruitment, for the pirates needed able seamen and skilled craftsmen more than ever after taking casualties. The dead of both sides would be thrown overboard without ceremony. Given the sorts of wounds inflicted in sea battles and the kind of care injured men received, the wounded might very soon envy the dead.

Though the term 'butcher's bill' may have originated in a later age, it applies equally well to the toll of shipboard casualties suffered on both sides during a determined attack by pirates. A battle aboard a vessel at sea was in many ways worse than one on land, for it was more concentrated. The mutilation and murder of small-arms fire, round shot, grape shot and fragmenting grenadoes were multiplied where sailors were crowded together on narrow decks. Surrounded by water, men struggling hand to hand against their enemies had little room to manoeuvre and almost no place they could flee to. Boarding pikes with pyramidal heads punched wounds that were difficult to close, while a quick twist of a flat-bladed pike driven home produced a similar result. Cutlasses and axes hacked into men's bodies like meat cleavers. The wounds could be horrific. Captain Philip Lyne was marched to his trial in 1726 with his wounds untended. According to a contemporary newspaper account 'he had one eye shot out, which with part of his nose, hung down on his face'.

Surgeons were valued additions to pirate crews, and were recruited or forced to join whenever possible. But in that era a surgeon was not at all the same thing as a physician or our modern doctor. At best he was a medic who might have plenty of practical experience dealing with wounds of all sorts. At worst, he was little more than a barber or even the ship's carpenter, who was handy with a saw. For shattered limbs there was usually only one treatment – amputation. And even if the patient managed to survive the cutting, probing and stitching – all done without any better anaesthesia than rum or a bullet to bite on, and performed in filthy surroundings – then the next hurdle was infection or even gangrene. The butcher's bill continued to mount for days or even weeks after the battle.

Meanwhile, aboard the captured merchant ship, the pirates still remaining on their feet began the methodical, if often frenzied, process of looting.

## PLUNDER

Another great pirate myth is that their plunder consisted of pieces of eight, chests of precious jewels and bars of gold. While the rich prizes of pirate fiction such as treasure-laden Spanish galleons did exist, and had fallen victim to Elizabethan sea dogs or Dutch privateers in previous centuries, by the early 18th century the days when these could be captured were long past. The Spanish still shipped gold and silver from the New World to Spain in their annual treasure fleets, but these powerful squadrons were too well defended, and pirates left them well alone. The wrecking of the treasure fleet in 1715 presented unscrupulous seamen in American waters with a unique opportunity for plunder, but this was very much the exception.

What might have motivated potential pirate recruits were tales of the rich hauls of plunder that were garnered by the 'Red Sea Roundsmen' of the last

In August 1720 the pirate Edward England captured the British East India Company ship *Cassandra* off Johanna Island in the Indian Ocean. His men later deposed him for being too lenient with his victims.

decade of the 17th century. These pirates preyed on the richly laden pilgrim ships sailing between India and the Muslim ports of the Red Sea, and men like Thomas Tew and Henry Every managed to seize a fortune in plunder – acquired in the form of coins, jewels and gold dust. However, those days too had passed. By 1710 at the latest these pilgrim ships regularly sailed in convoy, escorted by warships belonging to the British East India Company; this put them beyond the reach of the handful of pirates who still operated in the Indian Ocean. These men had to be content with lesser prizes, although the most lucrative of these – East Indiamen – were occasionally captured, yielding a small fortune to those pirates brave enough to take on these heavily armed merchantmen.

This left the normal merchant shipping that plied the waters of the Caribbean, the Atlantic, the Indian Ocean or the West African coast. These were the ships carrying cargoes such as rum or sugar from the West Indies; tobacco, cotton, timber or furs from North America; slaves from Africa; wine, spirits or manufactured goods from Europe; or cloth and spices from India and the East Indies. Certainly there was money to be had – often a reasonable quantity of it. The captains or pursers of most merchant ships of the period carried small money chests on board, which were used to pay the

In this evocative illustration the pirate captain Henry Every has some stolen jewels appraised. Every was spectacularly successful in his looting of the Mogul pilgrims returning from Mecca. Illustration by Howard Pyle, 1887.

Charles Vane was a diehard pirate who refused to accept a pardon in August 1718 and continued his attacks until he was deposed by his own crew. He was eventually captured, tried and executed in Jamaica.

crew, settle port dues, bribe officials or cover the cost of repairs. These money chests were claimed by the pirate quartermaster, and the contents kept 'in common', to be divided up between the pirates at a later date.

Apart from money, other goods on board a prize were highly valued by pirates. These included charts and navigational devices, weapons, clothing, tools and fittings, new sails, tobacco and salt. The other great hauls were drink and provisions, the two staples that helped to guarantee a happy pirate crew. Cargoes of claret, madeira, rum, gin or brandy were usually drunk then and there, unless the pirate captain could convince his men to postpone their revelries until they were safely out of harm's way. These were effectively seen as consumable cargoes, to be enjoyed by the crew, rather than held in common for division later on.

The problem was what to do with any other type of captured cargo, such as sugar, cloth, timber or slaves. To turn these goods into hard cash the pirates had to sell them to a merchant who was willing to do business with them. That meant they needed a friendly port – something of a rarity in the period. New Providence became an entrepôt for pirate plunder, as traders willing to deal in stolen goods made their way to this growing shanty town in the Bahamas. This gave pirates the chance to sell their cargoes, which were then smuggled into ports in the West Indies or North America and sold on for a substantial profit. This marketplace was finally closed to the pirates in August 1718.

Every other port was closed to them, with the possible exception of a few harbours in colonial North America or West Africa, where there was no permanent European authority backed up by a garrison or a naval guard ship. Blackbeard may well have been trying to develop his own base at Bath Town, North Carolina, but he was killed in battle before his operation in the Outer Banks was fully established. Another option was to anchor in some deserted bay or island in the Caribbean and deal with passing trading vessels. William Kidd did just that in 1701, though he was a privateer, not a pirate, and was ultimately hanged for crimes he didn't commit. This form of backwoods trading was a dangerous practice, as word could easily reach the authorities and a warship be sent to deal with the pirates. This is what happened to Thomas Anstis when he was surprised by the Royal Navy off the Cayman Islands, and indirectly to Bartholomew Roberts, who was holding slave ships to ransom when Captain Ogle appeared, commanding HMS *Swallow*.

This meant that when pirates captured a prize, the cargo was often of no value to them. In most cases the pirates were content with rifling through the ship for money and drink and then letting their victims go. At other times they deliberately ruined the cargo, slashing bales of cloth, throwing sugar cane over the side or landing slaves on the nearest uninhabited point of land. They might even force the merchant seamen into the ship's boat and then set fire to their vessel, cargo and all.

While much of this wanton destruction was an attempt to strike back against profiteering ship owners and merchants, it was also a symptom of the lack of control over a pirate crew. They were able to enjoy an orgy of wanton destruction, especially after the quartermaster had deemed the cargo worthless, as nobody had the power to stop them. Once again, Captain Snelgrave was on hand to witness the scene. He said of Howell Davis' men that during the pillaging of a prize ship they 'made such waste and destruction during their pillage that a more numerous set of such villains would, in a short time, have ruined a great city.' From the pirates' perspective, if you couldn't eat it, drink it, smoke it or spend it, plunder was of absolutely no value to them.

Howard Pyle's *So the Treasure was Divided* captures the spirit, if not the details, of pirates dividing the spoils. Pirates operated on a shares basis, often with the captain receiving only two shares compared with a crewman's one.

Howard Pyle reaffirmed both the popular image of pirate captains dressed as gentlemen and that of buried treasure in his *Kidd at Gardiner's Island*.

# REVENGE

In 1718, the Boston sea captain Thomas Checkley was captured by pirates, and during their later trial he claimed that they pretended to be 'Robbin Hoods Men'. In other words, like the legendary medieval outlaw, these pirates saw themselves as performing a useful social service by stealing from the rich and giving to the poor. This was not uncommon. A similar line shines through the trial records, testimonies by victims and accounts of final speeches from the gallows. The majority of pirates had severed their links with society, and in the words of Captain Johnson were 'at war with the world'. By linking their robberies to a greater cause, they were trying to justify their crimes in the eyes of the world, while indulging in what they saw as revenge against penny-pinching shipowners, tyrannical sea captains and unscrupulous merchants, who were seen as the oppressors of the common sailor. As they saw it, they were out for revenge.

Pirates are shown in this early 19th-century illustration 'sweating' a prisoner – probably a merchant captain – as a display of revenge against this figure of authority and what he represented, or, more mundanely, to extract information about any hidden cache of money.

This idea of vengeance is reflected in the names the pirates of the Golden Age of Piracy gave to their ships. Several pirates called their ship the *Revenge*, while there was also *Fame's Revenge* and the rather more unusual *New York Revenge's Revenge*. Blackbeard's flagship became the *Queen Anne's Revenge*. Clearly this wasn't a coincidence, but part of a general trend, where pirates sought retribution against what they saw as an unjust system.

On 1 April 1721 Captain William Snelgrave's slave ship, the *Bird Galley*, was captured by pirates in the Sierra Leone River. When attacked, the crew refused to fire back, for fear of retaliation from their pirate captors. The pirate quartermaster approached Snelgrave, furious that he had ordered his men to fire. The quartermaster shot at Snelgrave and wounded him, before clubbing the captain to the deck. He tried to escape, but he was cornered by the pirate boatswain, who clubbed him again. At that point Snelgrave's crew intervened, shouting: 'For God sake don't kill our captain. We never were with a better man.' That impromptu testimony was what saved Snelgrave's life.

He should have considered himself lucky. In many cases the pirates demanded what they called 'the distribution of justice', and if the merchant captain was found to have maltreated his crew he could be beaten, humiliated, tortured or killed. A favourite amusement was 'sweating', where the captain was surrounded by jeering pirates and forced to run round and round a mast while a fiddler played a lively air. To encourage him his tormentors would prod him with their swords or knives, and the sweating would continue until the captain dropped from exhaustion or the pirates became bored with the amusement. It has been said that this humiliation represented the vicious circle of the seaman's life, and was therefore a particularly apt expression of revenge.

In 1719 the pirate Howell Davis once claimed that the reason his crew embraced piracy was 'to revenge themselves on base merchants and cruel commanders of ships'. Two years before, in March 1717, when Sam Bellamy in the *Whydah* captured a prize off the coast of Virginia, he reputedly made a lengthy speech justifying his actions to a merchant captain. While Captain Johnson's account of this may be apocryphal, it certainly highlights the depth of feeling felt by most pirates of this period. Bellamy told the man:

Though you are a sneaking puppy, and so are all those who will submit to be governed by laws which rich men have made for their own security; for the cowardly whelps have not the courage otherwise to defend what they get by knavery; but damn ye altogether; damn them for a pack of crafty rascals, and you, who serve them, for a parcel of hen-hearted numskulls.

They vilify us, the scoundrels do, when there is only this difference, they rob the poor under the cover of the law, forsooth, and we plunder the rich under the protection of our own courage... You are a devilish conscience rascal, I am a free prince, and I have as much authority to make war on the whole world, as he who has a hundred sail of ships at sea, and an army of 100,000 men in the field. And this, my conscience tells me, but there is no arguing with such snivelling puppies, who allow superiors to kick them about deck at pleasure.

This same theme of revenge and war against the world was repeated by the pirate William Fly, who was hanged on the Boston waterfront in July 1726. It was common to allow condemned men to make a final speech from the gallows, as they were usually remorseful, which pleased the crowd and the attendant preacher, who in this case was the Reverend Cotton Mather. Fly was far from penitent, however, and he seized the opportunity to issue a last warning. He demanded that: 'All Masters of vessels might take warning by the fate of the Captain [Captain John Green, killed by Fly] that he had murder'd, and to pay sailors their wages when due, and to treat them better; saying, that their barbarity to them made so many turn pyrates.' While the great upsurge of piracy had passed, the grievances felt by many pirates of the Golden Age of Piracy had still not been redressed, and so men like Fly still felt that they had cause for revenge.

While this desire for revenge was clear, some pirates were clearly psychopathic, and their actions had more to do with sating a lust for wanton murder than anything else. In late 1722 Edward Low captured the *Wright Galley* off the Azores, and, according to Johnson, 'because at first they showed inclinations to defend themselves and what they had, the pirates cut and mangled them in a barbarous manner, particularly some Portuguese passengers, two of whom being friars, they triced up at each arm of the foreyard, before they were quite dead, and this they repeated several times out of sport.' The cook on board a French prize fared even worse: 'Who, they said, being a greasy fellow, would fry well in the fire; so the poor man was bound to the mainmast, and burnt in the ship, to the no small diversion of Low and his mermidons.'

The killing or injuring of sea captains was only one manifestation of this demand for vengeance. When Bartholomew Roberts was operating in the Leeward Islands in 1720 he raided the roadstead of St Kitts and burned all the vessels in the harbour. This was done in retaliation for a recent hanging of pirates on the island. Similarly, when the French governor of Martinique sent warships to hunt him down, Roberts saw this as a personal insult, and swore revenge on the governor and his island. The story goes that he captured and hanged the governor, but this is another apocryphal embellishment by Captain Johnson. He did, however, offer a reward for the head of the man, in retaliation for the price set on his own head. As the pirate crews of the Golden Age of Piracy were hunted down one by one, the remaining pirates frequently swore revenge and threatened to wage a war of reciprocal terror. It was little wonder that the European and colonial authorities did whatever they could to rid the seas of this pirate threat once and for all.

# FATE

When Bartholomew Roberts proclaimed that as a pirate he expected 'a merry life and a short one' he knew what he was talking about. He knew perfectly well that the odds of survival were stacked against him, and were shortening with each month he remained at large. The rise of piracy following the end of the War of the Spanish Succession certainly alarmed the authorities, and colonial governors from the Leeward Islands to Newfoundland petitioned the British government for help. When it came, the response was particularly effective – a carrot-and-stick policy, where a pardon was offered to those willing to mend their ways, followed by a brutal campaign of extermination against those who remained at large. For Roberts and those like him, there would be no leniency.

This policy was implemented in several ways. In the first place all known ports were closed to pirates, or anyone suspected of piracy. Then, government authority was imposed on the Bahamas, to deny the pirates their base on New Providence. Naval patrols were stepped up, with warships posted to cruise off known pirate 'hot spots', or to protect the approaches to major colonial ports or settlements such as New York, Philadelphia or Jamaica. The final stage would be more proactive – sending warships or expeditions to extirpate known pirate crews. All these measures led to the death or capture of a substantial number of pirates. They in turn led to the next all-important

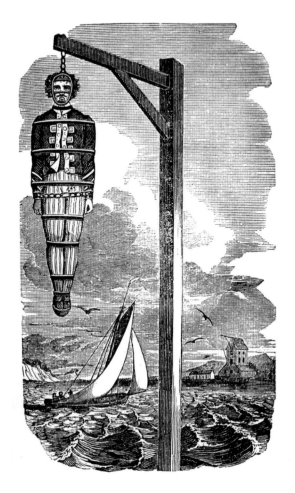

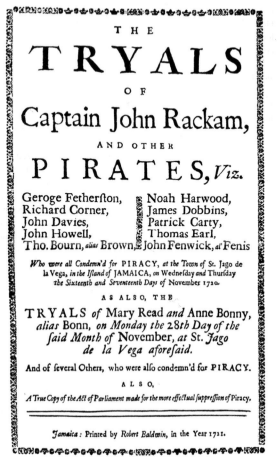

THE

# TRYALS

OF

## Captain John Rackam,

AND OTHER

# PIRATES, *Viz.*

| | |
|---|---|
| Geroge Fetherston, | Noah Harwood, |
| Richard Corner, | James Dobbins, |
| John Davies, | Patrick Carty, |
| John Howell, | Thomas Earl, |
| Tho. Bourn, *alias* Brown, | John Fenwick, *at* Fenis |

*Who were all Condemn'd for* PIRACY, *at the Town of St. Jago de la Vega, in the Island of* JAMAICA, *on Wednesday and Thursday the Sixteenth and Seventeenth Days of November* 1720.

AS ALSO, THE

TRYALS *of* Mary Read *and* Anne Bonny, *alias* Bonn, *on Monday the* 28th *Day of the said Month of* November, *at St. Jago de la Vega aforesaid.*

And of several Others, who were also condemn'd for PIRACY.

ALSO,

*A True Copy of the Act of Parliament made for the more effectual suppression of Piracy.*

*Jamaica:* Printed by *Robert Baldwin,* in the Year 1721.

part of the government plan – the very public trial and execution of these pirate captives, and the widespread vilification of them and their crimes. The aim, of course, was to discourage other sailors from following their example.

To use the words of the Reverend Mather, at the execution of some of Sam Bellamy's crew in late 1717, pirates were portrayed as *hostes humani generis* (the common enemies of mankind), hunted by all nations, and as 'sea monsters'. He added that anyone who even sympathised with these pirates was sinful by association. Almost exactly a year later, when Stede Bonnet stood trial in Charles Town, the colony's attorney general stated that piracy 'is a crime so odious and horrid in all its circumstances' that he and other officials were at a loss for words. In effect, these lawyers, preachers and officials were engaged in a campaign to strip the pirates of any support they might have in maritime communities, or from the common man.

In fact, piracy was a crime that was aimed at a relatively small sector of society. For the most part its victims were ship owners, merchants and sea captains who maltreated their crew. The buccaneers of the previous century had a far greater impact, burning whole cities, capturing treasure fleets and terrorizing large swathes of the Caribbean basin. The difference was that these men had limited their attacks to the Spanish, a nation that habitually closed its markets to other European nations. Consequently, the depredations of these buccaneers were serving a mercantile purpose, by damaging the economic interests of a national rival. A half-century later, the pirates who roamed the Caribbean, the Atlantic seaboard of North America or the West African coast were, as the attorney general of Massachusetts put it, causing 'destruction to the utmost part of our territories'. One wonders whether if Blackbeard had picked on Spanish rather than French, Dutch and British ships, he might have avoided becoming the target of a major anti-piracy operation and losing his life in battle with the Royal Navy.

The result of this vilification was that once captured, pirates had little chance of escaping the noose. In pirate trials, whether they were held in London, Edinburgh, Williamsburg, Boston, New Providence, Kingston, Charles Town or Cape Coast Castle, the defendants were denied the basic opportunity to defend themselves against the charges. This was in part because of the legal system of the time, when these trials were regulated by Admiralty law; the defendant was denied a voice, or at least he was refused legal counsel, and therefore had little chance of avoiding entanglement in legal niceties. In the trial of William Kidd in 1701, two lawyers were provided for him, but only to answer points of law – not to help him fight his case. Worse, crucial evidence that might have saved him was deliberately withheld by the Admiralty. As a result, a man who was almost certainly innocent of the charge of piracy was condemned to death.

Other pirate trials were surprisingly brief – most lasted no more than one or two days, even when several dozen pirates stood together in the dock. Most of these men lacked the education to be able to speak eloquently in their own defence, and anyway, the tendency was to condemn an entire crew and then to assess each individual condemned man to see whether leniency might be appropriate given mitigating circumstances. Some pirates escaped the gallows because they were able to convince the judge that they had been recently forced to join the pirate crew against their will. Others were spared because of their age, or, in the case of Anne Bonny and Mary Read, because of their sex, and the fact they were with child. These, though, were the exceptions. In the trial of 'Calico Jack' Rackam in Jamaica in 1721, the innocent turtle fishermen who had been carousing with the pirates before

Ironically, Woodes Rogers was a successful privateer in his early career before becoming governor of the Bahamas in 1717. He used pirates to capture pirates and break their power in the Caribbean. In this print, Rogers and his privateer crew frisk Spanish ladies for their valuables in a raid on Guayquil, Equador, in 1709.

*Captain Kidd on the Deck of the Adventure Galley*, by Howard Pyle. The Hispanic appearance of Kidd is notable, even amongst Pyle's depictions of pirates. Kidd was a pirate hunter rather than a pirate, although he was accused of crossing the line into piracy, and executed for it, despite a lack of evidence.

their capture were sentenced and hanged alongside the real pirates, as the judge was unwilling to listen to their pleas. After all, he was there to uphold the status quo as much as the law, which meant setting an example.

This policy of making an example of captured pirates was continued to its logical conclusion. Executions were public affairs, and pirates were expected to apologise for their crimes and throw themselves on the mercy of the Almighty. Pirates like William Fly were the exception – most meekly acquiesced, and even joined in singing a hymn before the final drop, singing, as some witnesses claimed, with clear, lusty voices. The hanging itself was usually a multiple one, with several pirates being executed at the same time. According to Admiralty law the gallows were erected below the high-tide mark, which marked the boundary of Admiralty authority. The pirates were rarely blindfolded, but their arms were tied, and at the appointed moment the platform they stood on was knocked away. Unlike later executions, the aim was not necessarily to break the neck – death would come slowly, as a result of strangulation.

After death, the bodies of the pirates were tied to stakes dug into the foreshore near the low-tide mark, and they were left there for the space of three tides, watched by a guard to prevent souvenir hunters from tampering with the corpses. Then in most cases the bodies were daubed in tar to preserve them, bundled into metal cages, and suspended on a prominent headland to serve as a warning to other would-be pirates for years to come. Between 1717 and 1726 some 418 pirates faced the gallows in this way, although the total may well be higher as many records are incomplete. The effect of this mass extirpation was self-evident. By the time Captain Johnson published his *General History* in 1724, the so-called Golden Age of Piracy was effectively

---

**H**    **JUSTICE**

On a cold morning in early January 1721, four pirates were hanged at Leith Sands, near Edinburgh in Scotland. One of the pirates, John Stewart, took the opportunity to give some last remarks. Stewart no doubt had given much thought to his speech, perhaps pondering his words long before his capture. For every pirate knew that a short career as a free rover followed by a rope halter was his likely fate. And though pirates frequently faced death in many forms, they seemed to have a special horror of public hanging. Perhaps it was the shame they dreaded, for hangings always brought out crowds of spectators from every level of society to jeer and celebrate. The humiliation continued even after death, for the bodies of hanged pirates were left to rot in chains on open display. Or it could be that from the pirate's perspective hanging seemed like such an unjust reward for choosing freedom, equality, excitement and possible wealth over a life of hopeless drudgery and poverty. Though many pirates who came to trial claimed (sometimes truthfully) that they had been forced into outlawry or were the victims of circumstance, most ended up like Stewart and his comrades beneath a gallows, with nothing left of their roving life but a few minutes granted for their last words. When they had finished, the cart was pulled from beneath their feet, leaving them hanging from the cross beam with their comrades.

**ABOVE**
Pirates were executed according to Admiralty law, which meant that the punishment was carried out below the high-water mark, as the foreshore was deemed to be within Admiralty jurisdiction. The execution shown here was carried out in Wapping in London, on the foreshore of the Thames.

**ABOVE RIGHT**
The hanging of the pirate captain Stede Bonnet in Charles Town (Charleston) in November 1718. Two months earlier Bonnet and his men were cornered by pirate hunters in the Cape Fear River, and captured after a brief sea battle.

over. While the trials and executions would continue for another two years, the governments of Europe and colonial America had achieved what they had set out to do. They had won their bitter decade-long war against the pirates.

# PIRATE RESOURCES

## Museums and galleries

### National Maritime Museum, Greenwich, London
Britain's premier maritime museum has a superb collection of paintings, prints and drawings from this period, as well as weaponry, navigational equipment, charts and maritime equipment. Its library contains logbooks of warships engaged in anti-piracy operations, and the original edition of Captain Johnson's *General History*.
www.nmm.ac.uk

### National Archives, Kew, London
What was once the Public Record Office houses a wealth of documentary information, including trial transcripts, Admiralty records, reports by colonial governors, period newspapers, ship logbooks, journals and original descriptions of several pirates of the Golden Age of Piracy. It is probably the best resource in the world for the serious pirate researcher.
www.nationalarchives.gov.uk

### Museum of London, London Wall, London
This museum collection includes artefacts and records relating to the imprisonment, trial and execution of pirates in the British capital.
www.museumoflondon.org.uk

### Mariners' Museum, Newport News, Virginia
The 'Mariners' is the American equivalent of Britain's National Maritime Museum, with a superb collection relating to America's maritime past. Their collection of ship models, paintings, charts and documents helps breathe life into the period.
www.marinersmuseum.org

### St Augustine Pirates and Treasure Museum, St Augustine, Florida
Originally founded in Key West, Florida, the Pirates Museum moved to St Augustine in 2010, to a venue that is better suited to interpreting the story of piracy during the Golden Age of Piracy through a combination of artefacts and dramatic pirate-themed displays.
www.thepiratemuseum.com

### Pirates of Nassau Museum, Nassau, Bahamas
A colourful and evocative interpretation of New Providence during its pirate heyday. The museum contains a replica of a pirate sloop, waxwork tableaux of pirate scenes and even a pirate tavern.
www.pirates-of-nassau.com

### The North Carolina Maritime Museum, Beaufort, North Carolina
In 1996, the wreck of what is almost certainly Blackbeard's flagship *Queen Anne's Revenge* was discovered off Beaufort, North Carolina. The shipwreck has been painstakingly excavated, and the conserved artefacts are displayed and interpreted in a new purpose-built gallery, which also tells the whole story of Blackbeard, his ship and the excavation.
www.ncmaritimemuseums.com

### Whydah Pirate Museum, Provincetown, Massachusetts
Built around artefacts from Sam Bellamy's pirate ship *Whydah*, this museum was founded as an adjunct to the Whydah Expedition, the ongoing excavation of this important pirate shipwreck. As a result, the museum provides visitors with a fascinating insight into life on board a pirate ship during the Golden Age of Piracy.
www.whydah.org

### Delaware Art Museum, Wilmington, Delaware
This important art museum holds a superb collection of paintings by the artist Howard Pyle, including many of his best pirate paintings, including the superbly evocative works *Marooned* and *So the Treasure was Divided*.
www.delart.org

## Pirate events
These are just a selection of the pirate-themed events and festivals around the world. More details are available at www.piratefestivals.com.

### Pirates in Paradise Festival, Key West, Florida
A lively celebration of pirate history, myth and culture, this annual festival in late November combines scholarly lectures on pirate history with re-enactment, art exhibitions, a pirate market and a lot of carousing in the harbour bars.
www.piratesinparadise.com

### Pirates Week Festival, Cayman Islands
A celebration of Cayman's pirate heritage, this long-running festival held each November is when Grand Cayman lets its hair down, with a week of pirate-themed events.
www.piratesweekfestival.com

### Blackbeard Pirate Festival, Hampton, Virginia
A celebration of the world's most notorious pirate, this annual festival held in July includes a re-enactment of Blackbeard's last fight, and a pirate ball.
www.blackbeardpiratefestival.com

### International Talk Like a Pirate Day
22 September is 'Talk Like a Pirate Day', a tongue-in-cheek celebration of piracy that owes more to Robert Newton's portrayal of Long John Silver in Disney's *Treasure Island* than the pirates of history. Still, it is a day of good harmless pirate-related fun. Arrrrrr...
www.talklikeapirate.com

# FURTHER READING

Baer, Joel, *Pirates of the British Isles*, History Press: Stroud, 2005

Burg, B. R., *Sodomy and the Pirate Tradition*, New York, 1983

Clifford, Barry, *The Pirate Prince: Discovering the Priceless Treasures of the Sunken Ship* Whydah, Simon & Schuster: New York, 1993

Cordingly, David, *Under the Black Flag: The Romance and the Reality of Life among the Pirates*, Random House: London, 1995

Cordingly, David (ed.), *Pirates: Terror on the High Sea, from the Caribbean to the South China Sea*, Turner Publishing: Atlanta, 1996

Cordingly, David and Falconer, John, *Pirates: Fact & Fiction*, National Maritime Museum: London, 1992

Earle, Peter, *Sailors: English Merchant Seamen, 1650–1775*, Methuen: London, 1998

——, *The Pirate Wars*, Methuen: London, 2003

Johnson, Captain Charles, *A General History of the Robberies & Murders of the Most Notorious Pirates*, Conway Maritime Press: London, 1998 (first published London, 1724)

Konstam, Angus, *The History of Pirates*, Lyons Press: New York, 1999

——, *Blackbeard: America's Most Notorious Pirate*, Wiley: Hoboken, NJ, 2006

——, *Piracy: The Complete History*, Osprey Publishing: Oxford, 2008

——, *The World Atlas of Pirates*, Lyons Press: New York, 2009

Little, Benerson, *The Sea Rover's Practice: Pirate Tactics and Techniques, 1630–1730*, Potomac Books: Dulles, VA, 2005

Menges, Jeff A., *Pirates, Patriots and Princesses: The Art of Howard Pyle*, Dover Publications: Mineola, NY, 2009

Pyle, Howard, *The Book of Pirates*, Dover Publications: Toronto, Ontario, 1921 (reprinted 2000)

Rediker, Marcus, *Between the Devil and the Deep Blue Sea: Merchant Seamen, Pirates and the Anglo-American Maritime World, 1700–1750*, Cambridge University Press: Cambridge, 1987

——, *Villains of all Nations: Atlantic Pirates in the Golden Age*, Beacon Press: Boston, 2004

Rogozinski, Jan, *Pirates! An A–Z Encyclopaedia*, Da Capo Press: New York, 1995

# GLOSSARY

**Brig**  A two-masted vessel, with a square-rigged foremast and a fore-and-aft rigged sail on the lower mainmast.

**Buccaneer**  Originally a hunter from Hispaniola, the term later applied to European seamen who attacked the Spanish in the Caribbean basin during the mid- to late 17th century.

**Doubloon**  A Spanish gold coin, worth two escudos, and weighing 16oz.

**Letter of Marque**  A privateering commission or licence, drawn up between a sea captain and a European power, permitting him to attack the wartime enemies of the issuing government.

**Maroon**  The act of casting someone ashore on a deserted island and leaving them to die.

**Piece of eight**  A Spanish silver eight-real coin, weighing 8oz. It was used as a standard unit of currency for much of this period. Also known as a silver dollar, it was worth roughly half of an English silver pound or a Spanish gold escudo.

**Pirate**  A seaman who commits robbery at sea.

**Privateer**  An independent armed vessel, authorized by letter of marque to attack the shipping of an enemy power in time of war. Her crew were usually called privateersmen, or privateers.

**Prize**  A captured ship.

**Ship**  A three-masted vessel with square-rigged sails on all her masts. The term is also applied to encompass any large seagoing vessel.

**Sloop**  A single-masted vessel with fore-and-aft rigged sails.

**Spanish Main**  Officially the Caribbean coast of South America, but the term was also used to encompass all Spanish-owned territory in the Caribbean basin during the 16th–18th centuries.

# INDEX

References to illustrations are shown in **bold**.
Plates are shown with page in **bold** and caption
in brackets, e.g. **13** (12).